TWENTY-SIX WAYS to ESCAPE the WILES of the DEVIL CONCERNING MARRIAGE

Rev. Juan M. Young

TABLE of CONTENTS

(THE MENU)

UNIT ONE		THE COMPLIMENTARY BREAD or PEANUTS	4
		Introduction	4
	Chapter 1	Keeping Your Vision Clear of the Enemy's Intent	6
UNIT TWO		THE APPETIZERS	12
	Chapter 2	The Importance of Deleting Pride	12
	Chapter 3	The Need for Self-Control over Spouse Control	15
	Chapter 4	You Have Need of Patience	20
	Chapter 5	Noticing the Efforts of Your Spouse	23
	Chapter 6	The Apologizing Spirit	25
	Chapter 7	Passionate Sacrificing	28
	Chapter 8	Listening After Removing Stubbornness	31
	CHapter 9	Accepting Differences	34
	Chapter 10	Respecting Your Spouse and Their Privacy	36
	Chapter 11	Being Humble, Unselfish, and Thankful at the Same Time	40
UNIT THREE		THE ENTREE'	43
	Chapter 12	Showcasing Understanding	43
	Chapter 13	Baggage Claim and Avoiding the Trigger	46
	Chapter 14	New Family Adjustments	49
	Chapter 15	One Way Street Parenting	51
	Chapter 16	Overcoming Poor Communication by Asserting Good Communication	54
	Chapter 17	Balancing Family, Work, and Church Life	57
	Chapter 18	Managing Damage Before it Happens	60
	Chapter 19	Preparing for the Enemies of Massive Intent	62
	Chapter 20	Building on the Solid Foundation	65
UNIT FOUR		DESSERT	68
	Chapter 21	Building Strong Support After the Foundation	68
	Chapter 22	Praying with and for Your Spouse	70
	Chapter 23	Brag on Your Spouse and GOD to Edify and Not Create Jealousy	72
	Chapter 24	Maintain What You Have and Do Not Look Back	75
	Chapter 25	Handle All Necessary Business and Finish Strong	77
	Chapter 26	Finish Strong and Be Happy	81

Introduction

In the beginning, everything started off so romantic and so beautiful. The marriage proposal was elegant, and the wedding ceremony and reception was one for the ages. But when soon-to-be divorced couples prepare themselves for the inevitable breakup, the only thing that comes to mind is often pain, grief, and regret. The question may have often been asked, "How did we or how did I get here?" But the significance of the question should be broken down as to, "What did we do to prevent us from getting to this point?

The answer may very well be that those thousands or in some cases millions of dollars were spent on the formal ceremony of two joining in Holy Matrimony, while dollars and loose change were spent on the development of the marriage hypothetically speaking.

Many times, you might hear, "This person thinks that they are Holier than thou". But the term Holy is misinterpreted as it often is. Being Holy is not an attribute. It is a state of being. Holy is defined as: dedicated or consecrated to GOD or a religious purpose; sacred. If we were to under-define that definition, it would be Holy is simply being set aside to be used by GOD.

Matrimony is the ceremonial service concerning marriage. Marriage becomes holy matrimony when people dedicate and focus on honoring God and serving the other spouse at the same time. Both spouses must agree with this notion. Because once you make this commitment, both individuals are also committing that before GOD, other witnesses, and each other, that you two agree with GOD, his purpose for marriage, as well as his guidelines for marriage.

Once accepted, this is now your Covenant with GOD. Notice I did not say vow. Ecclesiastes 5:5 states, "Better is it that thou shouldest not vow, than that thou shouldest vow and not pay." Meaning do not make vows and promises before him and witnesses and don't keep them. But instead, he wants us to understand marriage and agree with his expectations of marriage which is our Covenant. Vows have been hand picked and earthly created. But our Covenant with GOD has been settled in Heaven.

Whether married at a church, courthouse, beach, or in front of just your Pastor or Bishop and two witnesses, the marriage is your Covenant and agreement. with GOD. Once we agree on anything with GOD, the invisible hunter "the devil" does not agree with it and will stop at nothing to break you from your Covenant with GOD. This will also break the union. He tries to do this by using his arsenal of wiles (tricks) as weapons of destruction.

This book is broken down into four units that are classified and presented as The Complementary Bread or Peanut Service, The Appetizers, The Entree, and The Dessert. The twenty-six chapters will break down how the enemy uses upbringings, trauma, society, selfish ways, idolatry, witchcraft, and misleading interpretations of GOD's expectations of marriages amongst a slew of other tactics that cause mishaps in marriages.

Understand that you are not alone! Both GOD and the enemy take the Covenant seriously. The question is do we as GOD's people take it seriously enough. Once we understand that this is spiritual warfare, we will fully understand how GOD is giving us grace through JESUS CHRIST, by teaching us through his life and his dealings on how to navigate through the things of this life and through our marriages.

12 "Beloved, think it not strange concerning the fiery trial which is to try you, as though some strange thing happened unto you:"
13 "But rejoice, inasmuch as ye are partakers of Christ's sufferings; that, when his glory shall be revealed, ye may be glad also with exceeding joy."
1 Peter 4:12 & 13

By the end of this book, I hope that GOD shows us through the Word of GOD how we are to effectively "Counteract" against the wiles of the invisible hunter. My faith and desires are that it will help those considering marriage, those that are struggling in marriage, and for those that are on the right track, by encouraging them to go even further!
Let us pray...
"Let the words of my mouth, and the meditation of my heart, be acceptable in thy sight, O Lord, my strength, and my redeemer. Amen!"
(Psalms 19:14)

Unit One:

The Complimentary Bread and Peanuts

Chapter 1: Keeping Your Vision Clear of the Enemy's Intent

"And the LORD said unto Satan, Whence comest thou? Then Satan answered the LORD, and said, From going to and fro in the earth, and from walking up and down in it." (Job 1:7)

Be sober, be vigilant; because your adversary the devil, as a roaring lion, walketh about, seeking whom he may devour:
(1 Peter 5:8)

"And the Lord said, Simon, Simon, behold, Satan hath desired to have you, that he may sift you as wheat:" "But I have prayed for thee, that thy faith fail not:
(Luke 22:31 & 32)

These scriptures represent only a portion of the evil desires of Lucifer Satan. He also has come to steal, kill, and destroy, but he is not after stealing your car and your house. Neither is he after destroying your kids and your marriage. But his intent is to steal, kill, and destroy your faith. If he can get the faith, he can devour the rest.

If he can effectively get to the faith, then marriage is his next intent. Because a fallen marriage has the potential to cause long term effects on the car, the house, the kids, and a relationship with GOD.

But naturally many of our visions have been compromised long before we have stepped inside of the marriage building. As kids, many have unfortunately seen some things that clouded their minds and visions about marriage. Some predicted or predetermined what would happen or what they would not allow to happen once they became of age. Others were taught things based upon personal feelings and biased opinions instead of biblical principles.

From the time that we have been of school age, we have been of age to learn the perspective attributes of growing into young men and women and also equipped with the knowledge to be molded into GOD-Fearing husbands and wives. Ecclesiastes 12:1 reads in the NLT Version, "Don't let the excitement of youth cause you to forget your Creator. Honor him in your youth before you grow old and say, "Life is not pleasant anymore." But some of these environments prophetically overshadowed GOD's way by hindering, and negatively impacting the development of minds that caused youths to grow up and miss out on the blessings and pleasantness of life and marriage.

If Satan clouds the mind and vision, he can affect the order and truthful propositions of GOD's design. Proverbs 18:22 says, "Whoso findeth a wife findeth a good thing, and obtaineth favour of the LORD." So in actuality, it's not GOD's intent for a woman to search for, look for, or solicit to find a husband. A woman was already designed for a particular man.

"And the LORD GOD caused a deep sleep to fall upon Adam, and he slept: and he took one of his ribs, and closed up the flesh instead thereof;" "And the rib, which the LORD GOD had taken from man, made he a woman, and brought her unto the man." Genesis 2:21 & 22

This signifies that the Creator had descriptively and metaphorically surgically removed a rib from the side of Adam to create his helper Eve. Give close and thoughtful attention to this. Eve was not created from the front of Adam, that she should lead or usurp authority over him. Neither was she created from his back that she should detest or abhor him. But she was designed specifically for Adam from Adam's side. Distinctively level and close to his heart right underneath his arm to insinuate side by side. By being, bone of his bone and flesh of his flesh, Adam and Eve were now to be united side by side in every way as husband and wife. Designed to give themselves totally and wholeheartedly to one another.

Eve was ready when it was time to receive "her rib". And this should alarm women to work on themselves until GOD is ready to cause a sleep to come down on the specific man that's of GOD's choice.

Both men and women should be continuing to work on themselves if it is prior to marriage or even after they have married. Truthfully, all single ways should be or should have been worked on prior to marriage, but blurred vision will distort thoughts into believing that one can flick on a switch and those single thoughts, behaviors, and ways will just disappear like that.

Blurred visions and thoughts will also cause confusion and cause eyes to be spiritually blinded by looking at physical stature or outward appearances of men and women in either good ways or bad ways. When Samuel locked in on one, when he was sent by the LORD to Jesse's sons to see which one had the anointing of the LORD in 1 Samuel 16:7, "The LORD said unto Samuel, Look not on his countenance, or on the height of his stature; because I have refused him: for the LORD seeth not as man seeth; for man looketh on the outward appearance, but the LORD looketh on the heart.

Satanic wiles concerning witchcraft and Idolatry will also cloud vision when it comes to making decisions in life and in marriage. Deuteronomy 18:10-12 in the NLT informs us,
10 For example, never sacrifice your son or daughter as a burnt offering.[a] And do not let your people practice fortune-telling, or use sorcery, or interpret omens, or engage in witchcraft,
11 or cast spells, or function as mediums or psychics, or call forth the spirits of the dead.
12 Anyone who does these things is detestable to the Lord. It is because the other nations have done these detestable things that the Lord your God will drive them out ahead of you."

There's danger in witchcraft and the same is to be said concerning idolatry. Idolatry is defined as the worship of someone or something other than GOD as though it were GOD. The first of the biblical Ten Commandments prohibits idolatry: "Thou shall have no other gods before me."

Astrology is a form of idolatry and is a refusal to acknowledge GOD and his sovereignty. The Bible is firmly clear that GOD is the One who created us in his image. He is also the one who gives us our personality in which he has made each one of us uniquely different. On this earth, there is nobody else like you. Psalms 139: 1-13 further explains and details the prior.

Each zodiac sign contains a wide range of elucidations that are inadvertently showcased about a person. With such a large variety of descriptions, it is easy to believe that a few of the descriptions may be somewhat truthful about a few people born in a specific birth date range.

Zodiac Signs and astrology myths not only present GOD as a shallow minded stereotypical power, but they place a limit on the overall projectile and trajectory of the possibilities of many concerning marriages. In following these myths, Zodiac seekers believe their Zodiac sign determines if they are compatible for such said relationship status. Whether it is a sibling relationship, parent/ child relationship, friendship relationship, or an intimate relationship. According to their description, if you were born in a certain month or have a certain sign, you are or are not supposed to have a connection.

GOD has created and designed us uniquely differently. Even when it comes to identical twins, twins or their family members are often asked, "How can you tell them apart?" Usually the twin or a family member follows up with, "this twin has this mark or feature and that twin doesn't."

GOD is not to be placed inside of a simple structured system developed by man that was inspired by evil forces. The structured system was inspired to psychologically persuade the people of GOD to invoke doubt and limit GOD's power in their perspective lives. Keep in mind that GOD's total power is limitless. But doubting GOD will limit the effectiveness of his power in a person's life. We will get a little bit deeper into the depth of the power of words and thoughts by us, the people around, and the forces of the airwaves in society a bit throughout in the upcoming chapters.

Zodiac signs effortlessly tend to use systematic and often forcible pressure causing men, women, boys, and girls to believe that a person born in a said month can not manifest outside of the said description from said forces. This is an eye-opening trick from the evil hunter.

GOD specifically said through Solomon in the book of Proverbs 21 in verse 1 that, "The king's heart is in the hand of the LORD, as the rivers of water: he turneth it whithersoever he will." This not only suggests, but it acutely clarifies that GOD is in control and has the power over any description that is painted or depicted of us by any force whatsoever.

Many have prayed or are praying for someone that GOD has possibly already sent their way but was rejected by them because of their belief in the "Astrological Way of Thinking." Afterwards, they claim that there are no good men or women around. There are good men and women that exist. It may be highly possible that they are in that not-compatible category categorized by the Astrology field which may have influenced a person to miss out on their GOD-given blessing.

The enemy is very crafty and is a craftsman of blurring vision. He's a visionary in his own evil right but has no dominion over our thoughts. The only way he is able to have control over our thoughts is if the power that's been supplied and invested in us isn't applied.

Often during the premarital years, many men and women struggle with secret and personal insecurities. These insecurities range from emotional distress, isolation, depression, personal growth limitations, and low self esteem.

Some may cross examine themselves whether or not they can show beyond doubt consequential emotional affiliations, which in turn can subscribe to a slothful advancement when it comes to their potential of personal development.

A person's sight has been dimmed when their self esteem is essentially zero to low. Low self esteem is characterized as a person that is extremely critical of themselves by downplaying or ignoring their positive qualities. They judge or belittle themselves to be inferior to those around them oftentimes by using useless or negative words to describe themselves such as dumb, stupid, fat, ugly, unlikeable, or unlovable.

Symptoms include lack of assertiveness by agreeing to things that may not be desired to be done. More symptoms align with and include a person thinking they do not deserve to be happy. They do not accept or reverse a person's compliment into a negative. They also avoid challenges for fear of failing. Self comparisons are often the results of some of these symptoms.

Whatever the cause, reasons, or symptoms of low self esteem in addition to single shortcomings, ways, and mishaps that are not handled prior to marriage will not be beneficial. But will instead be an impediment and hindrance to achieving the best outcome in marriage. No marriage is going to make a person become or feel more important, more pretty, more handsome, more intelligent, or become a better woman or man. A person must be fully checked-in spiritually, mentally, and emotionally as a single individual to hit the ground running and to eliminate unnecessary stress and pressure that will put strains and shackles on a newly crowned spouse.

The devil's intent is to start the marriage off sinking if he can not prevent the marriage from taking place. Not handling single issues will cause "Marriage Stability" in the initial stages to be drowned by "single issues". Once "single issues" have been identified, addressed, and resolved, recognizing and adjusting to the characteristics of marriage are now considered in play......

Unit Two:

The Appetizers

Chapter 2: The Importance of Deleting Pride

What is pride? Pride is defined as, "A feeling that you respect yourself and you deserve to be respected by other people." Pride is also defined as, "A feeling that you are more important or better than other people." (Arrogant)

Proverbs 16:18 states that, "Pride goeth before destruction, and an haughty spirit before a fall." Pride is ultimately un-christian-like behavior and has caused many destructions and falls in marriages. Pride is a spirit and does not care who it hurts, abuses, or causes to fall.

There are many characteristics of pride that present many, mini-behaviors. A prideful spouse can be taken as becoming or being arrogant. Exhibiting an "I don't care attitude," or demonstrating that the other spouse is beneath them. Pride does not care who it offends or which spouse it uses in any altercation. It also uniquely, builds walls in marriages, while it separates and pushes spouses away from each other. This behavior places a roadblock and puts a strong hold on communication in marriage, and cuts the potential for it to grow.

Pride indeed gives justification to the flesh to withhold from your mate, because of circumstances and/or anger. Ecclesiastes 7:9 states, "Be not hasty in thy spirit to be angry: for anger resteth in the bosom of fools." New aged Twenty-First Century marriages struggle in huge part to pride. "I'm not doing this because of this. I'm not doing this because of that." Proverbs 14:1 informs us that, "Every wise woman buildeth her house: but the foolish plucketh it down with her hands." Both men and women in marriages have possibly been guilty of this scripture. Proverbs 14:3 reveals that, "In the mouth of the foolish is a rod of pride: but the lips of the wise shall preserve them."

These mini-behaviors at the moment of altercations seem justified, sanctified, and initially feel right. But, we've really just been bamboozled by the invisible hunter. Further down in the same chapter of Proverbs, verse 12 firmly educates us that, "There is a way which seemeth right unto a man, but the end thereof are the ways of death."This can be what is considered to be, "The slow death of a marriage."

In order to prevent the death of a marriage, there must first be, "The Death of Self." Matthew 16:24 enlightens, "Then said Jesus unto his disciples, If any man will come after me, let him deny himself, and take up his cross, and follow me." To follow after Christ, one must first deny himself. To have a successful marriage, one or two must often deny themselves. This is not a sign of weakness, but signs of maturity and wisdom. Denying yourself swiftly moves self-centered behavior and thoughts and makes it much easier to focus on the concerns of your spouse. Try not to get wrapped up in how much you have done for the marriage in addition to your personal accomplishments inside of the marriage. The enemy uses this form of self-centeredness to cause a spouse to feel over accomplished in a marriage and shine the light on themselves in which Satan himself has placed you in a dark hole in your home. Keep in mind, "Let nothing be done through strife or vainglory; but in lowliness of mind let each esteem other better than themselves." (Philippians 2:3)

Dying to self isn't really a sacrifice and really shouldn't be such a strain in our everyday lives. The more you seek GOD's will and his heart, love will grow and abide. Dying to self and pride is truly motivated by and through love. This death also requires mercy. We must understand that as husband and wife, we are going to make mistakes at points in our lives. We must recognize that genuine mercy involves apologizing and forgiving; for a prideful individual never think that they are wrong, never think that they need to apologize, and blindly never think that they need to forgive.

In order to even get anywhere, love should be followed by humility. Humility means
"the quality or condition of being humble; modest opinion or estimate of one's own importance, rank, etc." I am reminded of how Christ showed humility even being the only begotten of the Father. The word says in Philippians 2:5-9, "Let this mind be in you, which was also in Christ

Jesus: Who, being in the form of God, thought it not robbery to be equal with God: But made himself of no reputation, and took upon him the form of a servant, and was made in the likeness of men: And being found in fashion as a man, he humbled himself, and became obedient unto death, even the death of the cross. Wherefore God also hath highly exalted him, and given him a name which is above every name:" Christ loved us enough to die for us, and GOD gave him a name above every name for that, his humbleness and his humility. One of the least things we could do is allow pride to die in our marriages and lives in general. Try it and watch how GOD will highly exalt you in your spouse's eyes.

Chapter 3: The Need for Self-Control Over Spouse-Control

What is self-control? Self-control is defined as, "the ability to control one-self, in particular one's emotions and desires or the expressions of them in one's behavior, especially in difficult situations." It is also furthermore explained as, "the quality that allows you to stop yourself from doing things you want to do, in which it might not be in your personal best interest."

Self control can be broken down into five major categories. These categories are also valuable keys to marriage in which the invisible Hunter will use against you if you don't maintain or display self control. The five major categories are anger, health awareness, bills, finances, and manners. Proverbs 25:28 states, "He that hath no rule over his own spirit is like a city that is broken down, and without walls."

Anger is sometimes necessary and at other times often misunderstood and misused. The Bible informs us to be angry and sin not. Many times, we hold grudges toward one another, while at times saying extremely mean things to intentionally hurt the other spouse. This is where the sin regarding anger kicks in. Holding anger too long, or getting angry too fast has an outpour of good people that are now residing in prison or in the graveyard. Instead of protecting one another against and from angry or disrespectful individuals, spouses when angry, turn against one another and deliberately inject unhappiness into their spouse's life.

Generally, we think that we are using anger to protect ourselves, but instead have opened the door for the roaring lion to create issues in the marriage. Punishing the one that you vowed to love, honor, cherish, and protect is not the solution to a problem. It only allows the hurting spouse to build a wall from being hurt again, in which the wall may not be easy to tear down. When anger with sin arises, the marriage is no longer winning. It is on the losing end. There are times to be upset. Have

15

your moment and keep your mouth closed until you are able and strong enough to address the issue with wisdom and without disrespect. Do not create this habit of being angry. Once started, anger is an extremely difficult habit to break. If spouses are not careful, the marriage will break before the habit.

Health awareness in marriage is also enhanced by having self-control. Often, men are generally not too interested in this area. This may lead to having a few issues in your marriage. There is a mental self-control key with health awareness as well as a physical key with health awareness. Face it. When we say, "I Do", generally our intentions are to live and share a long happy life together. Sometimes, the lack of self control with our health and lifestyles ultimately wavers and tends to waste the phrase, "Happily Ever After".

Men do not attend the doctor's office on the regular. Men would probably highly decline a visit, even if they were to receive an invitation through the postal service. This is where the wisdom of a husband should kick in. Men in today's universe are macho and tough and can see when a woman and/ or wife should be humble. But, husbands should remove the beam out of our eyes and humble ourselves to visualize and understand when GOD is using our wives to keep a check on our health, in which will keep an edge on our lives together.

Eating late and what we eat then sleep affects long term health. What we place into our bodies has a long-term effect. Our lack of exercise has a long-term effect as well. We are living in aging bodies day by day. This applies to wives as well.

Health to wives much of the time is equivalent to a husband's mindset to sports or his mindset concerning the bedroom. Although occasionally, marriages and husbands and wives vastly comprise crossing points and swap mindsets. Do not get me wrong, both sides value health, but on average, women value it just a "little" bit more than a lot.

Women and wives on the other hand, do not have to receive an invitation to attend the doctor's office. It is already in their schedule annually or monthly. Keeping a tab on health awareness is huge but can mentally have a satanic effect on the mind if it is overused. Wives at times, cause and make themselves sick, depressed, and upset by not having self-control about worrying too much. If the invisible hunter struggles to get you to succumb to an evil tactic, he will push you to succumb by overdoing a good tactic that will hurt you in the long run.

An overloaded mind is a tool from the devil's tool crib, and husbands as well as wives grab it and use it often. Worrying about things, we do not have any control over. A spouse with an overloaded mind, tends to latch out at the closest person to them, which is naturally their spouse. Therefore it is necessary to exercise and make use of self-control to prevent from having an overloaded mind. When you feel the worrying nature coming on: "Shake it off"! Feel the overload trying to barge in: "Shake it off"!

Ponder this. The roads where I am from in Michigan, have a tendency to do quite well in the summer and autumn seasons. Due to the climate and weather conditions in the winter, Michigan roads struggle at times throughout the winter and most definitely in the spring when the conditions change. The salt for the snow, the traffic from vehicles, and the wide range of temperature change from winter to spring at times causes the roads to crack under pressure. Even though the roads get repaired or replaced sooner than later, the damage has an immediate effect on vehicles and on the owner's check books. The same thing happens when the roads in our mental lives are overloaded. It causes damage and life changing impairment. Self-control prevents damage. Understand that when things arise in your life in different seasons of your life, don't worry, don't faint, and more importantly, don't crack under pressure.

Self control is critical when it comes to bills and finances. Bills intertwine with finances, and finances intertwine with bills. Both parties involved are very important when it comes to bills and finances; therefore, both parties extremely need to have unquestionable self-control. Having sufficient income and funds is instrumental, but honorably comes second to communication. Whether or not a spouse is working or not, every decision one spouse makes affects the other spouse in some sort of way.

Addictions and the lack of communication are generally the causes of financial distortions. An addiction is a persistent compulsive dependence on a behavior or substance. Meaning alcohol is an addiction if abused along with drugs, partying, shopping, spending, gambling, and buying fast-food all the time. Never sacrifice what GOD has already placed in your hands to be able to pay bills on time. Once you lose it, it is gone. Now you grieve yourself and your spouse also, by digging a deeper debt due to borrowing to catch up on what GOD originally blessed you with to handle obligations. On top of that, you now must pay the lender back.

All holidays come only once a year. There is no excuse to overspend and place your family in a bind. We must use wisdom in all things. Even when giving or trying to be a blessing to someone else. This can clutch on to the same repercussions as overdoing a good thing. Give positioning yourself to still be exceedingly on top of water. Do not expect the ones that you place yourself in a bind to help, to help you when you're underwater. You can not look and focus on them. When you look at your spouse or in the mirror, all your spouse or the mirror sees is you. It's tough, but it's fitting. This applies to family as well. Sacrificing is beautiful. Paying your tithes is sacrificing and it is ordained by GOD. It is a must. Sacrificing, when your family and their being is the sacrifice, is bad business. Do not lend if you can not do without it. Do not co-sign or place your name on anything that you can not be responsible to pay for yourself if something happens to the other party that you co-signed for. Not even your children.

Having manners is the fifth key of self-control. This is beyond "yes ma'am" and "no ma'am." This is beyond "yes sir" and "no sir" too. Let us begin with the positive. Saying please and thank you really goes an extremely long way. It activates with your tone. How did you ask for what you requested? How did you respond after you received it? How was your tone? Was it genuine? Was it mean and nasty? All these questions play a significant part in having manners. There is a cause and effect of how we respond and our tone by saying it and actions by doing it. How is your tone with your spouse? Do you respect, appreciate, and honor your spouse, or do you disrespect them, raise your voice, treat them, or talk to them like a child? The way you treat and talk to your spouse changes the atmosphere of how they view and do things for you.

Teaching your children manners is a way of edifying your marriage as well. You ultimately train your children as they learn from watching the two of you. Teaching and making sure that your children respect your spouse is indeed a must.

Bad manners consist of numerous things. Spouses should learn how to clean up behind themselves. Husband's, if a wife is a stay-at-home wife, helping her out embarks and travels up her "He Loves Me" avenue. If you don't clean up behind yourself, she may view you as having bad manners. She may feel the need to tidy up daily or even donate a maintenance cleaning. Some wives tend to feel like a maid when they must restore a home daily. Husbands as well as children should chip in to enhance the wife's being. Less time for cleaning means more time for herself and you.

Wives and husbands both can make healthier and better homes by cleaning up behind themselves and by training children to do the same. Flush the toilet. Place the toilet seat back down. Clean hair out of the sink. Clean the sink and shower after usage. Press each other's clothes at times. Switch up washing dishes. Place soiled clothes in the hamper. Above all, ask your spouse about their plans or what you can do to help them.

Another bad manner is hygiene. Bad hygiene is implementing bad manners toward your spouse. Handle bodily hygiene in addition to oral hygiene. This type of behavior can cause a reproach from your spouse. Adequate soap, shampoo, and water along with ample amount of toothpaste on a toothbrush, contributes to good manners. Nose picking is not an option when there is tissue or Kleenex around. Prepared "passing gas" or "pooting or farting" is when you knowingly do it in front of your spouse. This causes a reproach as well. One may slip every now and then when you are awake or when you are sleep. Forced "burping" or "belching" is damaging also. Evaluate and see if and how this may be disturbing your marriage and peace. If it is, it is nothing that a little self-control can't and won't fix.

Chapter 4: You Have Need of Patience

Patience is, "the capacity to accept or tolerate delay, trouble, or suffering without getting angry or upset." Patience is something that is also not developed overnight. Married couples are inclined to expect immediate transformation within themselves and within their spouse, but theoretically, for the first two decades of your life or more, you were trained and/or practiced life as a single individual. The single life was your lifestyle. It takes more than a few days or a few months or years for a person to position themselves into a married type of a mind frame. A willing heart, determination, and the Word of GOD, will give you the only antidote to remedy this condition. After all, GOD is patient and consistently demonstrates patience with us daily.

Patience is needed with one another in general and in our everyday lives. Husbands and wives are going to have good days while not leaving out the bad days. Patience is needed in both, but "SUPERSIZED" patience is needed with your spouse when they are having a bad day. A spouse with a bad day psychologically expects their spouse to understand what they are dealing with. For instance, some wives that experience complications from conditions such as pregnancy, their monthly cycle, or menopause, expect to be comforted during these times. Other wives want and expect to be left alone. Some wives experience needing comfort, and in the self-same hour, expect to be left alone. A husband can feel caught in the middle and may eventually feel the pressure of trying to perform a balancing act concerning his spouse's moods.

Wives feel as though at times that all of their problems begin or end with a male. When a wife experiences MENstrual cramps or MENopause, the world to a woman shrinks and she may feel as though she is having a MENtal breakdown. Her emotions may make you feel as though you need to be on the go like a mail carrier to avoid your wife's discomfort. But just remember that the word mail is a heterograph word for MALE, so gear up for a variety of patience, because you are going to need it.

Husbands may test a wife's patience through many things. For illustration, if a husband has worked all week long and would like to relax on his off days, it may irritate or initiate a lazy attitude toward home and family. Often times this may test a wife's patience. A wife may have created a "Honey Do List" and has been waiting for it to be completed. As a husband, most of our intention is to start and finish the list. But things sometimes happen, and husbands generally hope and anticipate their wives to be sympathetic and not grasp and receive things personally. Men would like the same respect that women receive when they present to men that there are only so many hours in a day. At the same time, husbands should not have a slothful demeanor when their body is able and available to demolish the list.

As husbands, we have to be careful at times, that we don't allow our emotions to get deeply involved by being emotionally driven or more emotional than our wives. Either spouse shouldn't want to receive an award for being, "The Nagger of the Year". But there may be a problem if a husband nags more than his wife. That is not a knock or personal stereotype against women, but all throughout history even during the biblical days, women have always been more emotionally driven. But in all actuality, nagging should be non-existent in our marriages.

Displaying patience with finances and struggles is a necessity. In all obstacles of life, it is important that a spouse displays patience. This will in turn give the other spouse a little more room to make improvements while not leaving out progress. No one wants to walk on eggshells or hot rocks all of the time. Even if you perform pretty well under pressure.

Many couples individually proclaim, "I didn't sign up to be broke and struggle." And you would probably be right. But you did confess and sign up "for richer and for poor." You just may not have reached the richer part of your marriage yet.

You must believe to see. Proverbs 27:13 & 14, articulates that, "I had fainted, unless I had believed to see the goodness of the LORD in the land of the living. Wait on the LORD: be of good courage, and he shall strengthen thine heart: wait, I say, on the LORD." When you feel as though things are not going your way, and your strength is wavering, get a little Isaiah 40:31 in your system: "but they that wait upon the LORD shall renew their strength; they shall mount up with wings as eagles; they shall run, and not be weary; and they shall walk, and not faint."

Love is sticking by and showing your spouse that the two of you are going to make it. Finances may be tough, but "Charity suffereth long, and is kind; charity envieth not; charity vaunteth not itself, is not puffed up." (1 Cor 13:4) Be real about your love by distributing and allocating patience in all aspects of life with your spouse, because there is a need for patience for your marriage to survive.

Chapter 5: Noticing the Efforts of Your Spouse

Society has inevitably changed in so many ways. A lone way that it has not changed is that society's members love, soak up, and without certain delight in feeling and being appreciated. Many individuals in society enjoy giving and showing appreciation; although, to individuals who may not be as worthy as others. Husbands and wives fall short in this area, not realizing the gruesome aftermath that it presents.

Married couples daily go through days at a time giving compliments and showing kindness, while having an attitude for gratitude, seemingly like to everyone except their spouse. There are many ways of showing appreciation. But we would like to focus on observing and noticing the efforts of your spouse.

Efforts should be noticed and recognized in three different categories. When things are going extremely well, when things are not going so well, and also when a spouse is striving to make significant changes. Satan has blinded many couples of the importance of being observant.

Noticing effort denotes that you are paying attention to your spouse. The key is that we must recognize the bad as well as the good. But yet keeping a balance to submit or evaluate a diagnosis properly. Just like patience, you have to reference and understand that life changing efforts just don't happen overnight. You have to press through it like anything else in life, whether you're the one that is putting forth an effort to make change, or if you are the one that is trying to wait patiently for the change to occur. Both instances are efforts.

One of the greatest tricks submitted by the hunter is discouragement. Who does he try and use to get you discouraged the most? Almost undeniably your spouse is the answer. Do not give up if you become discouraged on either side. Galatians speaks of this in Chapter 6 and verse 9, "And let us not be weary in well doing: for in due season we shall reap, if we faint not."

Showing and recognizing effort only cements that you care, you value, and that you want your marriage to work. Whether big or small, any amount of effort is progress. At times in the Christian community when it is pertaining to money, we often shout "Be thankful! Every little bit counts." Although money and efforts are far removed from each other in categories, it should behoove us to eradicate a vague vision, and "Be thankful," because every little bit of "effort" indeed counts.

In St. Luke chapter 18, verse 35 begins to explain the story about the blind man that was sitting by the wayside. He heard that Jesus was passing by. He asked Jesus to "have mercy on him?" Many rebuked him that he should keep quiet and hold his peace. But he cried louder. Jesus then asks, "for the man to be brought hither." Saying, "What wilt thou that I shall do unto thee?" And he said, "Lord, that I may receive my sight." And Jesus said unto him, "Receive thy sight: thy faith hath saved thee."

We are all on life's journey, and Jesus is always passing by. We should cry out to him, even when the people around you don't want you to see the good or efforts in and from your spouse. Cry even louder as the blind man did. Remember that discouragement is of the enemy and is a veil that ostensibly covers and shields our eyes from seeing. Ask Christ to give you sight to see your spouse's efforts and he will because of your faith in him and because of the belief that you want to show in and to your spouse. And the people around you will glorify GOD along with you and your spouse as the two of you both place efforts in furthermore consecrating your union.

Chapter 6: The Apologizing Spirit

Wait a minute. Did this just say, "The Apologizing Spirit?" Why yes. And believe it or not, an apology or saying I am sorry goes a long way on this journey, but especially in marriage. Some might say, "Well I don't apologize, and I most definitely don't say I'm sorry." And you most definitely will have long lasting issues in your marriage,

Wise Christians and wise spouses know when to concede and understand that apologizing is not a form of being soft or displaying weakness. It is a form of solidification that is instituted in the upper echelon of marriages. Sincere and heartfelt apologies in due course take the sting and pain out of the particular hurtful gesture that offended and reinforces the foundation.

Apologies are a way to set the table to show that you were or are wrong, that you care, and that you want to make things right with your spouse. Rendering an admission of guilt or a request for forgiveness can even be a money saver. It keeps the tissue and Kleenex cost down. Many tears are often shed before apologies have been bestowed.

It may help with the electrical bill. When hurt or at odds with their spouse, most spouses go into the other room to watch T.V. and leave the light on so that the offending spouse can't get any sleep because of the shining light. Not only is the light and T.V. on in the other room, but chances are, the T.V. may be on in the bedroom too, burning more electricity.

You will save money on gas for your vehicle. By and large, when a spouse is wounded, they tend to drive right past their home to avoid the conflict, in which they find any and everywhere to drive just to stay away. The spouse who is on the hot seat may even follow this well-known procedure too. Money is also wasted on food, because both sides eat fast food when no one wants to be at home.

The only person that resides at your home during this time is Lucifer himself. Even if an apology is not rendered at first, empathize that GOD never empowered, authorized, or sanctioned either spouse to expel or evict the other spouse from the bedroom and/ or place of residence. Neither does he approve of the spouse that's hurt to excuse themselves from the room or residence overnight.

    The first thing to go after a disagreement or argument is communication. If too long of a period goes by without communication, the fellowship has now been broken. Shortcuts in life commonly lead to dead ends or to confusion. Earnest apologizing is fundamental. It is one of the few times in life where I think GOD permits us to use shortcuts. This shortcut only leads and directs you back to communication with your spouse. The quicker that you get back to common ground with your spouse, the quicker the passion in your bedroom resurfaces. Although this is another area that couples must strive towards and must press through. 1 Corinthians 7:3-5 conveys, "Let the husband render unto the wife due benevolence: and likewise also the wife unto the husband. The wife hath not power of her own body, but the husband: and likewise also the husband hath not power of his own body, but the wife. Defraud ye not one the other, except it be with consent for a time, that ye may give yourselves to fasting and prayer; and come together again, that Satan tempt you not for your incontinency."

    So don't let apologizing be without sincerity and do not allow it to be a crutch. The bible narrates to us about having a contrite spirit. Having a contrite spirit means having a remorseful spirit wherein its secondary meaning is, do not do it again. In our court system today, many judges base their sentencing on whether or not the defendant is remorseful about the acts or undertakings that were committed. Even though they may be guilty, as I previously stated, sincere apologizing goes a long way as in court. The judge may have compassion and submit a lighter judgment due to a sincere apology and a remorseful speech and remorseful body language.

    Even when Jesus was presented to a woman who was caught in the very act of adultery, as usual he showed compassion toward the woman. The great feat was that he didn't pass judgment against the most. Another action that held great magnitude was how he notified her that she was forgiven and to go and sin no more. When spouses render a request for forgiveness and obtain it, value it, take it seriously. But the key to developing the marriage is "don't do it again." Take into account that just because one accepts an apology, doesn't mean that they are granting permission for you to do it again. It means that they simply forgave you on behalf of good merit.

Chapter 7: Passionate Sacrificing

What is sacrificing? Sacrificing is the continuation of either a loss or something that you give up, usually for the sake of a better cause. This better cause in particular is sacrificing for your marriage. Sacrificing is a colossal way to improve our character and behavior in our marriages. Sacrificing is hard for some and comes rather easy to others. Sacrificing is a heart-wrenching battle to those where it seems to be hard but flows like a peaceful river to the ones where it seems to be easy.

When you sacrifice with wisdom, you undoubtedly compromise and forfeit how you feel and do what is best for the marriage. When you apply wisdom and sacrifice, you certainly please GOD. Husbands and wives should get into a habit of sacrificing, but strongly and vastly in wisdom.

Sacrificing is a form of giving and not just that. But it is also a form of giving-in when you don't even feel like it. This is certainly why a variety of spouses refuse to sacrifice. It begins as an emotional entity, but eventually grows into being selfish. Many couples don't want or even plan to give an effort, for believing that their giving has been forfeited and their time and giving won't be repaid. Luke 6:38 promises and says, "Give, and it shall be given unto you; good measure, pressed down, and shaken together, and running over, shall men give into your bosom. For with the same measure that ye mete withal it shall be measured to you again." And just imagine how much he will bless spouses for giving certain things up for the sake of their marriage. For he indeed honors marriages that he ordained.

You must sacrifice when you feel like it and when you don't. There should be a trade off when sacrificing is processed in a marriage.

There should be a 50/50 effort from both spouses or 100% outpour from both spouses to balance and enhance the usefulness of the marriage. There was a part in a gospel song that referenced and said, "Lord I'm running, trying to make 100 because 99 ½ won't do. In marriage, 60/40 won't work, 70/30 won't work, and 80/20 won't work. If a percentage is lower than the equivalent of 80/20, Lord have mercy, you should have remained single with that type of an effort. But patience and recognizing if the other spouse is striving to reverse those efforts is a plus in itself.

The reason why some percentages are low is because many spouses sacrifice for their family that is not currently living at the residence. They sacrifice for their kids and their jobs, but won't sacrifice for their spouse who is supposed to be a part of them. Spouses often bank on their spouses to always be understanding of the situation at hand. But truth-be-told, you shouldn't sacrifice for others more than you sacrifice for your spouse.

Husbands ought not to work on another woman's car, or anyone else's car, if he can't work on his wife's car. Unless there is an unfixable problem that he is not equipped to fix. On the other hand, wives shouldn't cook for another man or anyone else, if she hasn't cooked for her spouse. Do you see the importance? This leaves an easy opening for the one that is seeking to destroy your marriage. The enemy is a doctor at injecting infidelity issues into our veins if we are not careful. Put yourself in your spouse's shoes. How would it feel if your spouse did certain things to you? What type of an image would it imply?

There are holidays that you are going to have to sacrifice and share with your spouse. Don't get me wrong, you don't have to sacrifice. But if you value peace in your home, it is a compromising option. Many family traditions have persuaded, validated, and become the source of trouble in marriages. You may have the intention to attend every function, but sometimes it just does not work. Different likes as well as different lifestyles affect rational decisions and may influence many homes and the children in the home ultimately when family events take place. Sometimes you have to take a stand for what you believe in, even though it may be taken personally by family. Family may think that you are different or better yet mean. Don't read too much into it. You are just misunderstood. Sometimes it may be time to present the possibility of beginning your own tradition. Nothing should be truly taken away from this decision. Just look at it as you are building something new.

Chapter 8: Listening After Removing Stubbornness

What is stubbornness and what role does it play in marriage? Stubbornness is the opposite of being flexible. It is the act of holding onto a view or attitude, refusing to change, to the point of being unreasonable. It is also defined as being persistent, continuing in an unyielding and unwavering manner, also called being headstrong.

A great deal of unions may retain a dirty filter if it is evaluated appropriately. "It's my way or the highway." This belief has spoiled the success of marriages in the Twenty-First Century. Countless personalities might come to the conclusion, in their eyes, that women are against men. They also may have the persona that the world that we live in belongs to a woman now. Contrary to those thoughts, this world still belongs to not a male human being, but GOD. Men as well as women should just be thankful to be a part of it.

All in all, men and women should not blame the opposite sex for the failures in marriage. Throughout history, both have assumed their roles and unfortunately played their parts. Removing stubbornness is a hearing aid to, "The Deaf Ear'. A stubborn person has a bold temperament and almost ten times out of ten, has a tremendously problematical time listening at any point. A few characteristics of a person displaying stubbornness is that a stubborn person thinks that they know it all, and are generally known for rebelling against the truth, good advice, logical feelings, and most definitely for rebelling against correction.

You might have heard this at your job, once your kids have become of age, and probably in your marriage, "I'm grown. I don't need anyone telling me what to do." That is probably true in a stubborn person's mind. A wise mentor of mine once said, "We are only grown in the aspect of being old enough to know better." Very, very fitting, and true, because there are things that we know better, yet we still do. We have to listen to someone. GOD profoundly proclaimed that Christ is the head of the church and is the head of man. It doesn't say controller or chief president.

The key information is that GOD is the head of the husband, and in GOD's program, whether we like it or not, there is an order that he steadfastly holds us accountable for. Husbands first must remove pride, self, and stubbornness to be able to hear and listen to GOD. On another note, a husband's mind needs to be clear to receive the wisdom from GOD through his wife. Note that I said wisdom. Wisdom from GOD allows you to see when he is speaking through your wife, while not falling and yielding into an emotional trap that can sometimes be presented through the adversary.

Tough decisions have to be and must be made as a husband. His entire family is leaning, riding, and weighs on his shoulders. Even though the pressures of life can weigh you down at times, GOD never gave husbands the right to abuse their authority. You have to first be taught before you can teach or lead anything. When you look at professional or collegiate sports, very rarely does an organization or school hire a head coach or manager without having any prior experience. Although you generally don't have prior experience as a husband, GOD has created many ways that you can gain the knowledge necessary to be effective at your stand. In Psalms 107:20 GOD says, "He sent his word, and healed them, and delivered them from their destructions.

On the backside, if a husband is being led by GOD, make haste to reference your husband and listen. Frequent amounts of spouses have fallen catastrophically to, "you ain't my mama or my daddy. Technically they do not have to be, because that would be offensive. But if they are being led by GOD, you might want to listen because GOD is watching and holding you accountable.

In marriage, things never go completely accordingly as you would like them to. This may cause a severe problem in the mind of a stubborn spouse. They may even act out or show their frustration toward the other spouse. If you are the spouse on the other end of receiving the outbursts of frustration, relax, pray, and take it in stride until it passes over. Whenever you feel that your spouse is acting up at the present time, don't pray for GOD to punish your spouse, but instead pray for GOD to have mercy on them.

There is nothing like a spouse that listens and takes advice before it's too late. A host of members of society have heard wise counsel and refused it using their first and second nature. Some have lost many things including their mind, their freedom, and hurtfully, their lives for failing to listen. If your spouse loves you, loves their marriage, loves GOD, and loves having your best interest at heart, take heed and lose the stubbornness and the "my way or the highway" attitude. Listen and/or do what's best. It might just save your marriage or furthermore, your life.

Chapter 9: Accepting Differences

We all have differences about us. As hard as it is to believe, spouses begin their marriages with differences about them. But through the excitement of being married, differences are without certain overlooked. Married couples must realize and understand that once you discover that there are differences between the two of you, it doesn't mean that the two of you are not compatible. It simply means that there are differences between the two of you.

Differences are brought upon by the challenges of life, likes and dis-likes, goals and dreams, but predominantly by both spouse's upbringing. Nothing is wrong with spouses enjoying opposite things. Even though couples are considered one, GOD permits us to have different preferences. Could you imagine having the same taste buds? It just does not seem correct, let alone seem nowhere close to being politically correct. But if the differences are accepted by both spouses, it edifies why GOD's design is so unique and beautiful. Two human beings with different personalities that were on different paths are now striving to live as one.

Accepting differences just means that you are willing to love your spouse and grow through your differences. This form of a degree helps you to grow as if it were an educational institution as you must graduate through different levels of accepting your spouse in full. The completion of diverse levels helps you to grow as a person and helps your spouse also.

Think about this. You were raised by contrasting parents or guardians. Raised and had to abide by two sets of rules. Accustomed to two different lifestyles and were surrounded by asymmetric and varying characteristics in siblings, in addition to having converse dreams and goals.

Love will find a way through differences. Love will find a way through weaknesses and strengths also. Love is what connects weaknesses and strengths. If a spouse is weaker in a certain area, the wisdom of the situation is that if you are strong in that particular area, you now combine with your spouse to be at least competitive as a tandem. If you are the one that's weaker, acknowledge it and collaborate with your spouse and be effective at whatever you do. In certain cases, if spouses are both strong in areas or are both weak in areas, conflict will rapidly arise. Two strong personalities assist in a bumping of heads. Two weaker areas or personalities that are conjoined pour out passive natures.

More often than not, superstar filled sports teams rarely gel together and at times fail to even contend. Some of the best teams are made up of people that complement one another. Let's break it down a little further. If your job or family had a potluck, and everyone that participated all prepared and brought baked beans, it would be such a depressing gathering. Different dishes would present more excitement and more spice. The same is to be expected with differences between spouses. It creates more spice and excitement. In baseball, managers often make constant adjustments, to compete in the game or often make adjustments to win the game. Think like a baseball manager. If you are having trouble hitting a curveball, let your spouse pinch hit for you and knock it out of the park. You may have not been the hero, but you still won as a team, so celebrate together.

Chapter 10: Respecting Your Spouse and Their Privacy

An enormously high number of burglaries happen daily. These burglaries habitually set aside families to feel empty, abused, disrespected, scared, hurt, and angry. They may also feel as though that their privacy has been vacated or violated. When a spouse disrespects their spouse and disrespects their privacy, that spouse in particular may feel empty, abused, disrespected, scared, hurt, angry, vacated, or violated at certain points.

Respect has everything to do with what you say, how you say it, and the timing of which you say it. A tone of voice can cause things to escalate quickly or can cause things to evaporate to the point of being non-existent. Proverbs 15: 1 & 2 teaches, A soft answer turneth away wrath: but grievous words stir up anger. The tongue of the wise useth knowledge aright: but the mouth of fools poureth out foolishness. This may sound harsh to some but disrespecting a spouse and vacating their privacy is foolishness.

A great form of disrespect may come from within your own home from overlooked persons. Some of these persons are indeed the little people in our children or the same little children that have grown into young or grown adults. Parents and spouses allow children whether young or old to fall into a blind foxhole and never hold them accountable at times. Spouses, at no point in life, should overlook their children or anyone else and allow them to disrespect their spouse. If it is your first born son, mama's man-man, daddy's little girl, or whatever the case may be, respect is a requirement from children in marriage.

If any child, small or big, searches out and finds weakness in a parent, the parents will be at odds like two magnets of the same kind, because children will play you against one another. No child is ever permitted to speak negatively against your spouse or their other parent. Even if a biological parent is not present in the home, a small child or grown child should never be authorized to speak negatively against their biological parent or even what is considered to be their step-parent. A stern correction should quickly follow without a suggested remedy or any backtalk from a child. A child should never be allowed to walk around in the home and it be fine and dandy for the child to not speak to or have an attitude with your spouse. This will lead you down "destruction avenue". The code between parents is broken if spouses allow these types of behaviors.

Do not allow efforts, attitudes, or individuals from prior relationships disrespect, empower, and inject trouble into your marriage. When you get married, you hold fast to not allow anyone to enter into your circle. The invisible troublemaker uses any and everything to cause unhappiness in a marriage. Once he can cause grief in one area, he tries to start a snowball effect of misery, sorrow, and gloom. If children are involved through a previous relationship, do your very best without disrespecting your spouse to get along with the other parent. Attempt to do it for the child or for the children's sake. Your relationship may be cordial with an ex or your pages might be far from each other. Either way, honor the Kingdom and hate no one. Romans 12:18 says, "If it be possible, as much as lieth in you, live peaceably with all men. When you have done all that you can do, do not pressure or force the issue. Pray and let GOD work it out. He will work it out without there being a strain on all involved parties.

In the last chapter, we talked about having likes as well as dislikes. Some of our dislikes turn into what are pet peeves. Many couples fall victim to being aggravators in our own homes. If a spouse doesn't like something and we knowingly proceed to do it to upset them, this is borderline disrespectful and outright silly. The devil aggravates us enough and doesn't love us, so why does he need help from a loved one in a spouse?

Respect in finances is sincerely important. For almost everything in life, finances matter. When it comes to respect and marriage, financial obstacles matter! Obstacles are brought upon us by the lack of financial means, the withholding of financial needs, and the ability to water financial seeds. Find that fine median in the middle, where both sides won't feel disrespected. Some spouses handle money better than the other spouse. Some think that they handle money better than the other spouse.

Either way, a spouse should try their very best not to cause the other spouse to feel less than a man or a woman.

When I was growing up, there was a saying that quoted, "sticks and stones may break my bones, but words will never hurt." As I grew older, in my opinion, I found that saying to be completely false. Words hurt, sting, buzz, and will pierce you if you allow them to, especially when the negatively spoken words come from a spouse.

Regardless of race, upbringing, lifestyles, age, or any slight advantage, spouses should never look down on their spouse. At no time should a spouse treat their spouse like a child. Husbands should not treat their wives like little girls and wives should not treat their husbands like little boys. This is such brutal and disrespectful behavior that hurts unions today. In fact, not only does this type of behavior hurt unions, but it hurts parenthood also. When children pick up on the behavior, at times they think that they are equal with the spouse that is being treated like a child. Whether or not you think that your spouse's behavior appropriately fits, don't disrespect them! Pray, show them mercy, and treat them right. Never break the bond!

Husbands and wives must answer to one another. You are one body. Don't be disrespectful to your own body. In marriage, indeed you are both grown, and there are stipulations that each must abide by. One is by respecting time. Single people stay out all night long. If not working midnights, spouses should be home. Spouses should never be away overnight without the consent of the other spouse. Midnight presents another day. And generally, if a spouse comes home at or after this time, it presents a problem. Phone calls and phone conversations should come to an end by a certain time of night. Phone conversations with someone of the opposite sex should most definitely alarm the integrity bell in us to alert our spouse. A lot of issues come from bad communication or come from misunderstandings.

Misunderstandings are prevalent in marriages where spouses hold certain positions in the job field, political field, and in the spiritual field. Spouses must show respect for their spouses when their job has confidentiality concerns. Agents and officers, and political officials take oaths to keep certain things confidential. The position that your spouse has, holds distinctive pressure. Why add more pressure on top of more pressure. Don't feel like your spouse is undermining or emasculating you by purposely being secretive. They are only being secretive because that is what the position calls for.

If your spouse holds a precious position or is an officer at church, plan on your spouse not speaking about the business of the church. The business of the church should remain the business of the church. Things get misconstrued and confusing when too many individuals come across information. GOD as well as his business is sacred. Why get upset, break fellowship, and disrespect the privacy of your spouse's position simply because they want GOD's business to remain sacred as he asked for it to be sacred.

Confidential information is more effective when it is confidential. Privacy is more effective when it is respected. Spouses feel more appreciated and loved when their spouse respects them. The key component in marriage is GOD. GOD is love. Love respects. And spouses should always show respect to their spouse in everything because respect multiplies blessings from your spouse.

Chapter 11: Being Humble, Unselfish, and Thankful at the Same Time

What does being humble, unselfish, and thankful all have in common? They all please GOD, in the midst of giving stability in marriage. Many might say that being humble and unselfish are identical. I would agree that they are similar but are slightly different in the same notion.

What does humble mean? Humble means having or showing a modest or low estimate of one's own importance." When a person is humble, they hold a unique value in stature, and uniquely allow another person to speak well of them. Even when someone speaks well of a humble person, ideally it makes them feel uncomfortable in their world.

In the Bible, GOD often initiates the importance of humbleness and the end product it has concerning being blessed. Being humble will open doors. A wise person can see a prideful or not so humble person from afar off. Humbleness helps you to hear, listen, and see better. Proverbs 16:19 says, "Better it is to be of an humble spirit with the lowly, than to divide the spoil with the proud. He that handleth a matter wisely shall find good: and whoso trusteth in theLord, happy is he."

The lack of being humble has hurt people in general and has caused marriages to be hit extremely hard. Many doors have been closed in lives for the lack of being humble. Many positions at jobs have passed over many people. It has caused them to quit as well feeling that they deserve more or feeling that they deserved a position.

Opened doors concerning blessings have taken a hit. Although GOD has never left the blessing business, he doesn't open doors to bless a haughty, un-humble, or a selfish minded person. When there is a spouse in the home that never wants to be humble, the demons are always there edging that spouse on to dig deeper into their un-humbleness. But in reality, they're just blocking the flow of blessings from entering the home.

When a spouse is selfish, they truly lack understanding. The English thesaurus describes selfish as, "lacking consideration for others; concerned chiefly with one's own personal profit or pleasure." Selfish spirits close doors from blessings also. Being selfish eventually causes you to not be liked by people in all phases of life. When a spouse is exercising the ability to be selfish, they have actually formed an alliance against the fellowship with their spouse and have now chosen to operate as two instead of one. You may have not verbally said that you are separated, but your actions have spoken for you.

You must understand that if things are in order, GOD gives freely unto us. Married couples must work together, give together, and have the same agenda because there are blessings that GOD wants to sanction the couple's way, and they are called "together blessings. Even though Christianity is an individual walk, he consents unity for man and woman, in which you will only be able to receive certain blessings in unity. Note that tithe paying is to be paid by both spouses that receive income. If not, this will play a huge role in the unity not being fully blessed.

You've heard the phrase, "it's better to give than receive", and this is true. Couples must recognize the favor that they can receive when they give to GOD first and to one another. Couples should feel the joy of giving themselves freely to their spouse. Selfish spouses have their own agendas and set out to please themselves. Unselfish spouses constantly find and create ways and avenues to please their spouse prior to pleasing themselves. If the married society focused on pleasing GOD first, and then their spouses, unselfishness would abide and the selfish spirit would be buried in the backyard.

After humbleness takes off and selfishness is buried, it clears the way for a clear psyche to be thankful. At times as a nation, country or world, we choose not to be thankful. Many things travel through our minds, but thankfulness seems to slip our mind. Day after day passes without the acknowledgment of things, which becomes a habit and creates an ungrateful spirit.

If we are consecrated to amble around with legs, have eyes to see and ears to hear, we should be thankful. If we have a portion of life, health, and strength, we should be thankful. If your spouse comes home every night, don't be cocky or have an "I ain't worried" type of an approach". Be thankful! I know your spouse might have a few issues that bother you, but if your spouse is good to you, be thankful! If your spouse hasn't poisoned you and/ or doesn't chase you around the house with a weapon, be thankful.

The world that we live in is dwindling and if you can wake up next to your spouse that might have been upset with you the night before and have your life and all of your limbs in their correct places, be thankful.

If you're a spouse that looks in the mirror and quotes to the mirror, that "you get on my nerves", be thankful because if you get on your own nerves, it's highly possible that you may for lack or the better get on your spouse's nerves. They accept you through your issues, so diligently find and create ways to be thankful for your spouse. It's a form of validated behavior that strengthens the marriage.

Unit Three:

The Entree'

Chapter 12: Showcasing Understanding

Understanding is extremely vital when it comes to a hale and hearty lucrative marriage. When you are enthusiastic to comprehend each other, new revelation and hope will surface. You will without delay become thrilled to concentrate on your marriage.

Once you understand why your husband acts an assured way, or why your wife thinks a firm way, it will change how you feel about him or her, even though nothing has truly altered. Empathy will move toward an accompanying "we're going to make it type of a conduct, because of understanding different attributes of your spouse.

I cannot overemphasize the significance of consideration and understanding. If you are not an understanding person, patience and perceptive goodwill are now out the door. Understanding is a block, but even in understanding, you need to get understanding. Not having an understanding spirit can and will be detrimental to the success of a marriage. Understanding does expand both ways. When we put emphasis on "expand both ways", its main thread is regarding understanding our pasts, but not making excuses for the behavior.

Excuses from a natural man or woman desires acceptance from the natural man or woman, but in GOD's eyes, he is not accepting any excuses. In Luke 14 beginning at the sixteenth verse, JESUS begins to explain how a certain man made a great feast. Certain individuals were asked to attend the feast, but by one accord, they all began to make excuses. One bought a piece of ground to see. Another bought five yoke of oxen and desired to test them out. Another said, I have a wife now;

therefore, I can't come. All asked to be excused. In the rest of the chapter, you'll discover the importance of why excuses shouldn't be made.

Excuses do not solve problems or situations. Excuses create a surge that causes turbulence when it comes to showcasing understanding. We all have things that happened in our childhoods, upbringings, single lives, relationship/ married lives, etc., which shaped us to some sort of degree. Some have developed depression and "Mommy & Daddy" issues, while others have experienced or have trust issues stemming from infidelity, emotional abuse, substance abuse, physical/ domestic abuse, sexual abuse, racial abuse, or being unloved by feeling neglected or abandoned. The writer said in Psalms 55:22, "Cast thy burden upon the LORD. and he shall sustain thee: he shall never suffer the righteous to be moved." This declaration was made and proven on Calvary, when CHRIST pinned all of our past, current, and future excuses, issues, deficiencies, and troubles on the cross.

Often people say, "it's easier said than done", but although overcoming does not happen overnight, these things are important to a person's well-being and crucial to success in a marriage. Both parties have things that bother or nag them, so it is imperative not to apply too much pressure and have patience. The excuse is normally presented as, "I'm like this because of what happened to me or I'm like this because I didn't get or have this in my life.

"My childhood or the lack thereof is the reason why I'm this way". We all have something that can hold us back if we allow it to, but the key is perseverance.

Some of our issues should have been outgrown by now, but instead we invite the notion of what has happened & have embraced it as a "Generational Curse. Albeit certain circumstances & experiences have caused traumatic stages in life, don't allow the enemy to rob you of happiness in marriage and life in general.

Well how does all of that tie into, "Showcasing Understanding"? Glad that you asked! The invisible hunter has a sneaky way of causing spouses to feel misunderstood. Compassion is necessary in marriage, and if your spouse hasn't fully found the way of dealing with or handling things of their past, being available, open minded, attentive, as well as caring will oftentimes entice partners to open up some.

You don't always have to be "Mister or Miss. Fix it. Listening, hearing, and by showcasing understanding can significantly help with healing. Sometimes, a spouse just needs to gain enough trust to feel that "someone cares". Who should care more than a loving and caring spouse?

Chapter 13: Baggage Claim and Avoiding the Trigger

Whether by plane, train, or by bus when traveling, the baggage claim or luggage claim can be an egregious procedure. By this time after the flight or ride, a person just wants to relax, rest, and be happy. However, it's generally time to claim your baggage.

One would assume that once a couple becomes one, that all prior issues should have been addressed. Marriage is sort of like the traveling part as far as after marriage. You're just interested in relaxing, resting, & being happy instead of dealing with any portion of baggage. But as we touched on in the last chapter, "Showcasing Understanding" can & will go a long way.

Those trust issues, in addition to those hurtful, and painful traumatic memories when carried into different stages of a person's life are called what is known to many as, "Baggage". Even though "Showcasing Understanding" is extremely valuable in itself, avoiding triggers that can potentially cause a serious mental relapse to a companion go hand and hand just as a Dictionary and Thesaurus.

By being attentive prior to, a caring and devoted spouse should have discussed and discovered where their spouse's birthmarks and moles are. Ironically, their wounds and scars on the physical and emotional side should have been discovered as well.

Spouses using things discussed, mentioned, or discovered for self gain to elevate themselves for manipulation, retaliation, criticism, boasting, negatively glorifying, critiquing, or bullying is totally unacceptable behavior and is prohibited according to Romans 15:1. "We then that are strong are to bear the infirmities of the weak and not to please ourselves."

That's right! When spouses become vulnerable and open up, it's a form of trust and therefore should not be taken advantage of, abused, or violated. Demonic nature enjoys exploiting relatively sacred information and turning it into ammunition for the married to get back at, retaliate, or to hit the love of their life where it hurts.

To cause (an event or situation) to happen or exist is defined as "Trigger". For example, if a person is allergic to something, it is extensively or almost always caused by a particular situation, event, activity, medicine, or food that in turn caused or triggered an allergic reaction of some sort. Meaning that as unfortunate as the situation may be, what triggers often solidifies "cause and effect" procedures.

Husbands and wives should never enjoy being the cause that triggers a negative effect on their marriage. As much as couples may hate to admit it, there are certain things over their lifetime that have had an effect on them until it has been carried over into different features and exposures throughout their lives including relationships unfortunately to another relationship. To be simply put, it's nothing but an ole overstuffed bag of "Baggage"

Baggage in life is definitely not created overnight and needs to be fully understood that it doesn't become unpacked overnight either. These things travel and have developed from baggage to wounds, scars, and scabs and subsequently can become interchangeable in different orders as well. Just as when our fleshly bodies have wounds, it is hard for it to heal if one keeps picking at it or touching it. You can not expect a spouse to heal from their emotional trauma if you continue to bring things up or pick with their emotional scabs. It will quickly turn into a sore again.

Husbands and wives play unique roles in GOD's creation. It's like Royalty. But there are consequences when it is not treated as such. The First Epistle of Peter Chapter 3 and verse 7 says, "Likewise, ye husbands, dwell with them according to knowledge, giving honour unto the wife, as unto the weaker vessel, and as being heirs together of the grace of life; that your prayers be not hindered." According to Proverbs Chapter 12 and verse 4, "A virtuous woman is a crown to her husband: but she that maketh ashamed is as rottenness in his bones."

Husbands don't allow your prayers to be hindered. Prayer is the bridge that will take you to peace, healing, and wisdom amongst other things. Once that bridge collapses, so will things in your marriage. Wives don't be rottenness to your husband's bones. When bones rot, the blood flow to part of the bone is disrupted. This results in death of bone tissue, and the bone can eventually break down and the joint will collapse.

The key element in both is that neither spouse should be their spouse's trouble. Uplift and edify one another. Do not be the trigger to their allergies or the picker of their wounds. Honor one another and be hope for them. Shine so bright that when evil wickedness and powers, and not leaving out rulers of the darkness of this world try to come against your marriage, they'll all be blinded by seeing the GOD in the both of you!

Chapter 14: New Family Adjustments

Adjustments in life can be evaluated and processed as either good adjustments or bad adjustments. Now who classifies what are the adjustments that need to be made, will have two individuals moving in divergent directions.

Jeremiah 29:11 professes, "For I know the thoughts that I think toward you, saith the LORD, thoughts of peace, and not of evil, to give you an expected end." While married couples tend to want an expected ending that will maneuver into their favor, they often rebuke the notion of change. Change or adjustments may seem to be complicated or downright unnecessary, difficult, or seem as though GOD is punishing you. But his intentions are for us to embrace growth by making adjustments and receive that peace that surpasses all understanding that will lead to that expected end.

Starting, expanding, or blending a family can manufacture some challenges if not properly handled. Issues from traditions and customs of men and women have been proven to be demoralizing, detrimental, and potentially devastating to the core beatitudes concerning marriage.

Everything is not signified or should not be conveyed from your biological family's way of doing or thinking. Neither should those attributes be conveyed from former relationships, partners, or marriages. Just as every human being's fingerprints are different, your new family should have its own set of fingerprints. It brings about a profound specific identity and rationalizes the importance of your stand for your new family.

The family's steps should be built firmly on GOD, but keep in mind that those keys from your last family generally will not fit the things with the new family. "I'm used to doing things this way", or I saw things done this way", or even better yet, "My parents or ex used to do this or that this way".

Well quite naturally, it does not matter what materialized prior to a particular or current marriage. As spouses, the obligation should be very simple; dedicated to your person " Your Spouse", and the offsprings that now have obliged through the biological process or through the addition thereof through marriage.

We can't force what doesn't fit. More times than not, a marriage will find turmoil if it is forced. Do not cripple the marriage by forcing your marriage's toes into smaller shoes that were displayed in another family's being that you've obviously outgrown. Everyone's marriage material can not fit yours. GOD may have a different avenue for your marriage that will still give your marriage an expected end. Make your situation special, but don't cripple it. Stand on the principles of GOD, but indeed be well equipped to establish good faith in your own marriage and family.

Chapter 15: One Way Street Parenting

Many cities and small towns have streets and roads that have adopted "One-Way Road" or "One-Way Street" terminology. If you're not familiar with the term or phrase, One-way traffic (or uni-directional traffic) is traffic that progresses in only one direction. A one-way street is a street or road either facilitating only one-way traffic, or specifically designed to direct vehicles. One-way streets typically result in higher and/or better traffic flow as it's easier for drivers to possibly avoid encountering oncoming traffic or turning through oncoming traffic. There are typically fewer accidents and traffic jams when one-way traffic is presented.

In times or situations when individuals may have become confused, distracted, impatient, or possibly even intoxicated, those venturing down one-way traffic streets the wrong way in the past have caused chaos, accidents, injuries, or even death.

The devil has a crash course designed basically for our marriages. A disguised unique way that he uses to dislodge the success of a marriage is through parenting and kids. Whatever crack or way that he can squeeze through, he will most certainly do it.

The number one thing that should be done in a marriage/parenting situation is, everyone must accept who they are and know who they are. In the Twenty-First Century, so much has been made of the "Biological vs Step" aspect of the matter when it comes to marriages and family. When the term "Step" is installed into the forefront, whether it's "Stepmom", "Stepdad", "Stepbrother", or "Stepsister", it's generally as a coverup that signifies that one desires to make it known that there's a separation that distinguishes what or who's accepted or potentially who is rejected out of respect to a biological being. The same thing applies when it comes to "Half-Brothers" and "Half-Sisters". In a moment where a family should be blending and bonding becoming closer, Satan has used these terms as ways to pry families and marriages apart.

Again, GOD is not the author of confusion. There's no way that it's acceptable for you to quote on quote, "love a husband or wife", but don't love their children and that's whether they were born in your union or prior to your union through a prior relationship. The same phrase that is used for "Biological Children" should be used for that uncomfortable discriminatory term "Step-Children", "That child or those children didn't ask to be here". So that's why it's so important to do what's necessary to blend a family through love for the better or common good of the family's structure and well being. In no wise does this exclude kids in the situation. Kids must accept their parents and siblings as well.

Oftentimes we hear the phrase, "Parenting doesn't come with a manual". The Bible is the manual to parenting and being on "one accord" when it comes to parenting is "One-Way Parenting". One-Way Parenting consists of the same attributes as One-Way Street driving..... Better Parenting flow, fewer parenting accidents, and fewer parenting jams when one-way parenting is presented.

There's one-way or a Flat-Rate for all kids in a family household. If it's only biological children present..... "One Way". If it's adopted or step-children..... "One Way" still. This notion of "My Children", "Your Children", and "Our Children together" is a manipulative way of thinking that's been presented by the enemy. It births division when two parents should be walking together. It creates jealousy and displays favoritism towards siblings and causes discord.

The parenting manual describes and displays the turmoil that it caused and will cause in Genesis Chapter 37. Jacob favored his son Joseph, because he was his son of old age. But the favoritism displayed by their father Jacob toward Joseph, caused Joseph's brothers to dislike him and they plotted to do awful things to their brother because of their father's actions. Be careful not to cause division between your children. Love them all and treat them fair and right. It will work for you instead of against you.

Having One-Way Parenting directly helps to create one established plan for the household. One set of rules and one set of consequences. It creates a force for the common good. It leaves no wiggle room and if stood upon properly, it creates an environment and avenue of respect for both parents. Kids shouldn't be able to use one parent against the other parent. If one says yes, both should be at a yes. If one says no, both should be at a no. If you're not on the same page, decisions should be postponed if possible until both parents are on one accord. If not, the enemy will exploit the situation and turn everyone in the household into enemies, especially the parents. Stick to the manual and lean not to your own understanding. Stay on course with "One-Way Parenting", and avoid the unnecessary traffic jams and accidents in marriage.

Chapter 16: Overcoming Poor Communication by Asserting Good Communication

In the previous four chapters of this unit, utilizing communication skills had some type of effect whether it was good or whether it was bad. We have different ways of communicating and how we learned these types of ways to communicate have a fundamental effect on how we deem communication should indeed be translated.

For illustration, some people yell, some fuss, some isolate themselves, some become mute, some verbally express, and some write down their thoughts. Many think that their way of communicating is far superior to the way that their spouse communicates.

There is often evidence in a marriage where it warrants the belief that it is okay for family members or best friends to communicate for you in place of yourself. But ultimately, it's just a temporary fix or shortcut that will lead to a dead end; albeit, in some cases, counseling may be necessary to bring the two sides to a common line of communication. In the event that counseling is necessary, seek out spiritual minded unbiased counselors who have the best interest of the "Kingdom's Sake" that will in turn work on the two willing participants' marriage's behalf.

In marriage, participants regularly think that they have the solution to communication but lack empathy or emotional support that will connect them to their partner's reception of receiving what they may be dishing out verbally, emotionally, spiritually, and even sexually.

The dictionary defines "empathy" as; the feeling that you understand and share another person's experiences and emotions. Synonyms for "empathy" are kindness, generosity, compassion, tenderness, mercy, leniency, forbearance, and goodwill.

Lacking empathy, compassion, and understanding causes breakdowns, disturbances, and apprehensions with spouses and their communication desires.

One keynote to remember is that both spouses must be willing to communicate at that particular moment. Trying to force a grown individual to talk or listen when they are not in the headspace to talk or express themselves isn't healthy for either individual. Forcing anything in life that does not fit will burst or explode and generally doesn't work out for the good.

With that being said, the party or partner that wasn't in the headspace at the time should be willing to revisit the conversation when in the proper headspace if both spouses truly believe it's in the best interest of the marriage. Sweeping too many things under the rug will as aforementioned cause you to trip over that same pile more so sooner than later.

While we've mentioned about a spouse not wanting to talk at a particular moment, this is where empathy must be evaluated and shown towards the other's feelings. Some feel the need to block an individual from leaving their physical presence or they try to use verbal insults, manipulative verbiage, or fleshly inspired behavior to spark the spouse that is trying to retrieve into their mental safe place, in which the devil resurrects the blaze that was on the verge of dying down.

Part of this behavior reflects the emotional distress of "Over-Communicating". Over-Communicating is expressing to your spouse everything you desire, feel, as well as think. Not understanding that it is not necessarily a healthy communication style. It may cause your partner to experience or feel unable to meet certain expectations or demands, and it may possibly feel to that individual that you are accusing or potentially causing them to feel responsible for your erratic behavior, actions, and reactions.

Extremely too much communication about the same things, over and over again, can lead to massive arguments. When an overly aggressive or emotionally expressive partner essentially over-communicates — it can abruptly lead to the other spouse shutting down or uttering a few words that they possibly didn't mean in an attempt to shut down the conversation.

Most introverts tend to try to postpone a conversation or meeting. An Introvert's mindset uses contrasting and longer structured pathways than that of an extrovert's brain. Introverts are passionate and are very deep thinkers and need excessive time to reflect, rationalize, and calculate. Especially when there's a lot to think about and breakdown.

Whatever way we communicate, we should ask ourselves, are we communicating or responding with the speed of GOD, with the knowledge of GOD, and with the compassion of GOD? In order to have a more established experience with communicating, these toxic techniques or traits must be buried.

1) The Blaming Game
2) Using Frustrated Verbal Language and Body Language
3) Halting the Conversation without an Explanation of Why
4) Staying in your Lane with Certain Topics and Past Trauma
5) Getting Defensive Instead of Evaluating Their Intent
6) Speaking for Your Spouse or Speaking About Why or What They Will Not Change
7) Being a Basher and Being Too Unfairly Critical
8) Loud Talking or Over Talking Your Spouse
9) Gaslighting Your Husband or Wife
10) Creating Assumptions That Your Spouse Should Be a Mind Reader and Already Know Something

Begin with some of these pointers and watch how the communication between the two of you improves. In every situation, we don't have to be a hero and fix things or try to fix our spouses. Live right and focus on yourself. Be in the Will of GOD. Pray for your spouse and not about your spouse and watch GOD do something. Remember "Lay aside every weight" and "Cast your cares and burdens upon the LORD". Even in your beloved marriage!

Chapter 17: Balancing Family, Work, and Church Life

Some of the most important things on this side of the grave are Family, Work, and Church Life. If there was a "Dedication Pie Chart", many of our charts would drastically have differing percentage numbers when it came to our dedication to family, work, and church life. Although there is no clear structure in what percentage is deemed appropriate, the Bible clearly talks about all three categories with great essence. The Holy Spirit will surely guide us into the proper percentages if we take heed to his guidance.

Being that all three are so valuable, it would be extremely difficult to cancel either one of them out. If one of the categories are neglected for whatever reason, home can and will be a place of turmoil until such said is corrected.

Balance is important for husbands and wives. More times than not, couples will find themselves needing to choose whether to be complacent with their balance or have a tumultuous mindset to improve or implement more balance.

The easiest roadmap to balance for the three categories would be to simplify them by simply dividing this category pie into one-third which would be 33% for home, 33% for work, and 33% for Church life. As much as it looks to be balanced on paper, we know as well as the enemy knows that it doesn't quite work as it does on paper.

Some believe that there's evidence in the Bible that leans towards the order being GOD, church life, family, then work. Then some believe that there's evidence in the Bible that subsequently leans towards the order being GOD, Family, church life, then work. As we see in both instances, two have the same exact order, "GOD and work" But much discrepancy is identified between the second and third places leaving, "Family and Church life" seemingly to be without a secured spot.

Do not lose track and focus of the adversary. He can conquer if he can get the family divided. Especially when feelings, emotions, jealousy, self righteousness, and blurred understanding are involved. The majority of breakdowns in understanding are brought upon by the inability to effectively communicate.

When it comes to church life and family, communication from both spouses and in opportune times from the kids is in fact a serenity form of order. The timing and follow through of the communication are indispensable as well. I learned a phrase years ago that stated, "When we communicate and explain prior to, we're educating and setting the tone. If we communicate and explain after, we've created and have submitted an excuse."

For example, if a mechanic tells you about a problem while diagnosing it and tells you all of the risks prior to working on your vehicle, you've been educated to have all of the knowledge necessary. Now if the same mechanic didn't tell you about the risks prior to, and now something has gone wrong while working on the vehicle, it will more than likely sound like an excuse that's costing you more money. See the difference between communication beforehand and only afterwards?

Balancing church life obligations and family obligations aren't much different when differentiating how communication needs to be presented. With the help and guidance of the LORD and with the proper communication, the order of family and church life can be interchangeable. At times there may be a calling for family life a little more. Gather whatever is necessary to make the necessary adjustments or arrangements. Likewise, when there's more of a calling for church life at a given time, making the necessary arrangements and adjustments would be in order here as well!

Never knowingly neglect the three categories or GOD and if it's been brought to your attention that you are neglecting or have been, humbly evaluate it and see if the assumption is valid. Negligence concerning either of the four (GOD, Family, Church Life, Work Life) consequently causes spiritual division from our Covenant with GOD. Work life is slightly different for husbands and wives according to the scripture, but both should understand their biblical responsibilities concerning work inside or outside of the home.

When husbands and wives properly balance in a nutshell, it will keep the Invisible Hunter at bay from trying to invade the marriage from this area of concern.

Chapter 18: Managing Damage Before It Happens

Managing damage or damage control is when measures are taken to minimize or curtail loss or harm. For example, as soon as an exterminator discovers termites, they take the imperative steps to fix the problem before it spreads or expands. Some homeowners or business owners take precautionary measures such as preventative maintenance plans to protect against potential pest infestations.

The same characteristics should apply to marriages as far as a preventative nature. Some issues can be managed before any sort of damage can occur. The power to manage damage actually lies in the hands of both parties inside of the union.

The handling of situations plays a significant role in managing damage. Ponder this for a moment. When certain circumstances arise, consider other options instead of jumping to harsh conclusions. Satan has caused many issues in marriages by either spouse jumping to conclusions by making false assumptions, claims, or accusations. When emotions are flying high, you can escape a potentially damaging escalating argument by taking time to wisely think things through rather than pointing fingers or reacting out of pure emotion.

Another red-flag or alarming damaging state is managing our weaknesses before they turn into habits or addictions. Habitual behaviors that could possibly lead to addiction are alcoholism, pill popping, drugs, gambling, pornography, lying, and shopping are just to name a few. Either one of these addictions in addition to more can steamroll a marriage into a point of no return if it is not nipped in the bud. Just as playing with fire will get you burned, so will flirting, or playing with an addiction.

Another thought to carry along with you is that for every negative obstacle or experience that comes against your union, develop togetherness and create an entire boatload of potentially positive experiences together to cancel out that lone negative experience. By doing this, you will both be exercising your faith by speaking life and supplanting positive energy into your marriage.

Problematical concerns or better yet conflict don't have to result in separation, divorce, or the demise of a marriage. With spiritual eyes, the Holy Spirit will generally show us things before they happen or take place. Giving us the opportunity to manage or check ourselves before the wreck comes upon us. No matter how many times we read this scripture, one thing is for sure... His WORD is right! 1 Corinthians 10:13 states, "There hath no temptation taken you but such as is common to man: but God is faithful, who will not suffer you to be tempted above that ye are able; but will with the temptation also make a way to escape, that ye may be able to bear it."

He gives us managerial material and gives us a way out of disagreements, conflicts, and arguments. But we ignore the escape before things happen and allow the fleshly man or woman to kick in; furthermore, deactivating us from managing damage before it happens.

When managing damage before it takes place, there's one substantial element that should be evaluated when GOD has given couples a way out of conflict. That element is reinforcing to yourselves why you desire for your marriage to work. As long as you have a "why", you have hope and have something to strive and reach towards. The most valuable encouragement of marital achievement by a long shot is the desire to make the marriage successful, regardless of any circumstances, conflicts, or challenges.

Benjamin Franklin once quoted, "If you fail to plan, you are planning to fail!" If marriage participants fail to manage damage before it comes about, then couples are failing to place themselves in the position to be ahead of damage, instead of trying to clean up all the rubbish that the damage has created. Keep in mind that although these organizations are awesome, there are no emergency relief plans, Red Cross, FEMA, etc. for when disaster hits a marriage. Managing things before disaster strikes is your insurance. Never go into a marriage situation without it.

Chapter 19: Preparing for the Enemies of Massive Intent

In sports, one of the greatest advantages for some of the greatest athletes and teams is knowing their opponents. Part of knowing their opponents is evaluating everything about them. There are advantages in knowing your opponent likes and their dislikes. Knowing their strengths and their weaknesses. Lastly, knowing what ways that they plan to attack you.

There is generally an offensive side of sports and also a defensive side. Teams and athletes generally need to be well rounded concerning both sides to be successful in their respective roles.

In organized sports, we generally see who we are competing against. Ephesians 6:12 reads, "For we wrestle not against flesh and blood, but against principalities, against powers, against the rulers of the darkness of this world, against spiritual wickedness in high places." Understand that there's rank in Heaven and there's rank in Hell even when it comes to evil also.

In life and marriage, the devil does not fight us alone. He has many offensive strategies that target us especially when it comes to marriage. Many of his demons lurk around as hunters doing the work of their master.... To steal, kill, and destroy.

Think with me for a minute. If we are not fighting against flesh and blood, then we're fighting against evil spirits of wickedness and enemies that we can't physically see. JESUS said in St. John Chapter 14, "I will not leave you comfortless", and "the Holy Spirit will guide you into all truth". If we lean and depend on the Holy Spirit, it will guide us and show us the evil spirits of wickedness and what we're up against.

Evil spirits just don't do the work themselves; they jump inside of the tandem in a marriage and cause havoc. Self examination is constantly needed inside of a marriage. Feelings come and feelings go.

Look at how the marriage might have been doing fine the night before, and it's disorderly commotion the next morning until one spouse mentions to the other, "Well, somebody woke up on the wrong side of the bed." Chances are that the spouse in question slept on the side that they have for years, but an evil spirit crept in overnight.

At the first sign of feeling or recognizing an evil spirit, one must immediately, "submit themselves to GOD, resist the devil or his demon's tactics, and they will flee. All the while, the spouse that has the right spirit should be praying and touching in agreement that the spirit exits the premises instead of being critical of the struggling spouse by allowing the spirit to dwell and leap on them.

A wedding ring is not the marriage, but it symbolizes commitment towards one another and towards their covenant with GOD. The ring also symbolizes that you, your spouse, and that same covenant with GOD, should be the only valuables in the ring circle at the end of the day.

Yes, some of our circles should indeed be that small. The more individuals involved in something, the higher the chances that it will be more complicated.

Evil and enemies can sometimes show their faces in the form of people that you do not know as well as close people that you do know. At all costs, we are to protect and guard our covenant. Ephesians 6:16 profoundly states, "Above all, taking the shield of faith, wherewith ye shall be able to quench all the fiery darts of the wicked." If you are not familiar with the term, Fiery Darts are people, their words, their evil intentions, and/or their jealous motives.

Everyone that says that "I'm happy for you" aren't. Some will encourage you to leave or cut ties with your spouse while they are still married themselves or are building their own relationship in hopes of getting an advantage over you! They will be in a relationship and you will be single full of regrets because you took advice from a fiery dart.

Be extremely careful and watchful because fiery darts can and will come in the forms of parents, siblings, and children too. Whomever the enemy can use to try and put a blockage or fork in the road of GOD's plan is definitely in play in his eyes.

Staying close to GOD will keep you ahead of any and all enemies and their intentions. Enemies will forever fight against your marriage, but that does not mean that they have to prevail. You just continue to fight on for your marriage and your covenant with GOD.

Chapter 20: Building on the Solid Foundation

The footing and foundation are exceedingly critical and principal components of any structural design, building, or home as the two give stability to the entire structure. A faulty or failing foundation can be devastating and create problems that can cause significant damage to your home or building's structure, and if left unattended to, it can even be dangerous or even fatal in some cases.

A faulty foundation can create holes, gaps, and cracks that insects and bugs can use to enter into the home or building which can lead to an egregious infestation. Bad foundations can cause structural damage to your home, which can also lead to cracks in your walls, ceilings, and floors.

Once cracks have engaged in the foundation, it can cause water to seep into your home or building, which can lead to mold and mildew growth, and damage to your furniture, and further damage to the flooring, and walls.

Finally, a not so good foundation can decrease the value of your property and make it difficult to pass inspection or sell.

Marriage is marginally different and at this point, if all of the other steps have properly been considered and applied, the solid foundation to your marriage should already be established. Now it's time to build on that solid foundation.

If a marriage isn't built properly foundation wise, the marriage will experience holes, gaps, and cracks that makes it easy for the devil to come in. It also allows water damage to seep in, where it will create funguses, mildew, and mold issues whereas if not treated immediately, the marriage can and will be deemed condemned or likely unlivable.

Building on faulty foundations will only give you shelter temporarily. But that solid foundation will give you rest, sleep, and can save you money in the long run by preventing expensive repairs and damage to your marriage.

There is nothing like peace of mind. When a solid foundation is present in marriage, couples are able to have peace of mind and are able to enjoy one another and be best friends. The bond should be stronger than ever before. It makes resting easier, vacationing easier, and undoubtedly makes stress levels, anxiety levels, and health better in general. It is never GOD's will for us to be stressed, broken down health wise, or be full of anxiety, for again "His thoughts towards and for us are good".

Building on the foundation are your benefits from your labor. One benefit is that it's much, much, easier to meet personal challenges when you know someone has you covered and has your back. In most surveys, it is often reported that the level of support desired and received from their spouse is a huge driving force and determining factor in how well that spouse achieves their personal goals and dreams.

With the dedication and full support of a spouse, the other spouse feels secure enough and has more than enough practical and emotional assistance to attack and aim for their important endeavors in life, whatever they may happen to be.

Another benefit of building on the foundation is when a couple has been resilient together and have ultimately built the foundation together. If accurately identified, a couple will discern how it also tremendously helped their growth together.

Once your marriage has gotten through a lot of the marital curves and mountains, a husband and wife will start to embody one another and their pros will more heavily outweigh their cons. Note that once you have fully established and accepted your marriage with your spouse, your satisfaction for your marriage and spouse will easily showcase and lead to your admiration for your partner.

You will also discover how well your partner makes you better as well as you'll discover how well they strengthen and complement you. "Iron sharpeneth iron; so a man sharpeneth the countenance of his friend. (Proverbs 27:17) And what better way than your renowned best friend to take part in your full purposed development.

As a follower of the gospel and of Jesus Christ, marriage is not everything when it comes to life and joy but remember that one of the prime and central places that GOD gives us to discover and enjoy life, peace, happiness, contentment, and joy is within marriage.

Building on your foundation will help the two of you together to discover, develop, and fulfill your joint purposes for each other and for the Kingdom's sake. According to our faith, the ideal example of a husband and wife is a mirror of the relationship between Christ and the church. By knowing this, this concept should always be applied in the structuring of marriage after the foundation.

A spouse never completes you. You are only complete in GOD. But your wife or husband does bring security to you. Never place your spouse in the position of GOD by announcing that they are your completion. That is a quick way to cause damage to the foundation. When adding to your marriage's foundation, focus on these 6 "U's" and not "You's".

1) Uplifting
2) Understanding
3) Unity
4) Unabated
5) Unbreakable
6) Undefeated

If both husband and wife focus on being uplifting and understanding to further build their unity, it will establish them to be unabated or unmovable, unbreakable, and undefeated when it comes to the marriage. Love on one another until you've become soulmates through your built-in longevity and leave no question as to how your foundation was built and the results showing why....

Unit Four:

Dessert

Chapter 21: Building Strong Support After the Foundation

In the last unit, we talked in particular about what a ring in marriage symbolizes. We also talked about how dangerous and risky it was to invite people into our circles. Our focus now shifts to building support around our established foundations.

I have learned over time that living in a community is essential to keeping a marriage vibrant. This is generally only recommended once your covenant with GOD, each other, and the marriage's foundation is intact and strong enough.

I reference back and stand on the fact that too many individuals in or closely around your union can cause some form of tension. But the valued art of integrity is who and what value that is associated with other couples should be advised to be closely invested or involved with you and your spouse?

Therefore we need to be extremely careful and intentional about regularly connecting with like-minded couples. Couples that are willing to use biblical references, values, and facts over pure emotional and biased takes and opinions.

We were placed down here to serve GOD and help one another until the return of JESUS CHRIST. Spouses who indeed share a healthy, vibrant relationship are encouraged to fellowship and lean on their support system. But must also recognize that they have a responsibility to encourage and help other couples to thrive as well. It's called giving back.

According to Hebrews 13:4, "Marriage should be honored by all". And we should take pleasure in giving back by participating in supporting other couples. Whether it's planning double date nights. Watching another's couple's children while they get much needed alone time. Reading the Bible or marriage books together as a group, or lastly by attending couple events, conferences, or retreats.

Each couple may desire different things or would like to experience different things. Keep in mind that whatever the choice may be, the goal is to create a culture and community that inspires others to duplicate success. History has proven and produced more times than not, that if 9 people are successful, a 10th person that joins the other 9 is highly likely to be successful as well.

It is frightening and baffling how the mind can work against you in your most vulnerable and emotional moments. It often offers confirmation bias of your worst insecurities, causing you to suffer from emotional distress and other conditions when dealing with things alone. This is why Lucifer wants to design a plan to get couples to feel alone and get comfortable with isolation from their spouses and comfortable from being around like-minded couples.

Villages and cultures help to reconnect you to the external world while giving you the opportunity to focus on other people and interactions on a regular basis. Check-ins often lead to positive interactions. The conversation does not necessarily have to do with anything marriage wise, but the positive influence is medicine in itself.

Being around happy people is a medicine. "A merry heart doeth good like a medicine: But a broken spirit drieth the bones." (Proverbs 17:22) Laughter is a gift from God. Laughter is a great way to stay encouraged and positive spiritual fellowships are replica blueprints of how to support your foundation.

Chapter 22: Praying with and for Your Spouse

Praying is something that should have been done from the beginning. 1 Thessalonians 5:14 says, "Now we exhort you, brethren, warn them that are unruly, comfort the feebleminded, support the weak, be patient toward all men." Verses 16 and 17 says, "Rejoice evermore" "Pray without ceasing".

Even if we were ever at a point of being at odds with our spouses, we should have been praying still. We should have comforted the feebleminded, supported the weaker, and had patience towards our spouses. Instead, society through the enemy has taught how to pray at a spouse instead of praying for a spouse. "LORD fix him or her" or somewhere along those lines is generally how the prayer goes.

Ideally, there's no particular or standard way to pray, but as a gesture of gratitude to Our Heavenly Father, I'd encourage starting off by thanking him for your spouse and the things that he or she may do that are beneficial and that are blessings to you. Things do not have to be as well as they are. Sometimes the devil pushes to focus on the things that need work instead of focusing solely on the things that are well.

So, after showing gratitude, implement the execution of praying for your spouse's day, their health, and their work day. Be conscious to pray for their strength, their daily walk, including decision making. Finally, just to announce a few more, pray for peace, protection, their role as a husband/ father or wife/mother, their spiritual walk, and for the presence of CHRIST in your marriage.

Mutual prayers to reach the throne from both marriage participants benefit the marriage in further building unity and "team or us" mentality. Prayer won't discontinue the battle between the adversary and your union, but it will help you indulge in your spouse's team as prayer warriors going to battle. Finding more time to pray together will insert more peace and allow fewer instances to be at odds with one another. I've heard it said like this before, "When you're in the "prayer closet" being soldiers in a war together with your prayer warrior spouse, it's ultimately what keeps you from being in war against each other".

Praying for and with one another places barriers around the two of you. Prayer has monumental effects on a marriage even beyond the simple things that we regard as important. Praying with your partner and for your partner can even result in an enlargement of romantic allegiance, greater marital satisfaction, and even more heartfelt forgiveness.

It's a form of encouragement. There is nothing like encouragement from a spouse. Spouses have been blessed with unique gifts that were designed and designated to be showcased only for their designed spouse. Nobody can speak or talk to that inner man or woman like their significant lover. To receive that encouragement through prayer is a privilege and blessing in itself. It builds clarity. It builds confidence. It builds a special bond that's called intimacy.

Intimacy is a close, familiar, and usually affectionate or loving personal relationship with another person. Intimacy is built up over time, and it requires patience and effort from both partners to create and maintain. Intimacy does not always mean sexual. Intimacy refers to a level of closeness where you feel validated and safe and when escorted in because of prayer, I must say that there aren't many greater feelings.

In marriages, four types of intimacy are hugely important: emotional, physical, mental, and spiritual. Once the spiritual intimacy is intact, it unlocks the doors to the other three. When intimacy is built through prayer, it allows husbands and wives to be completely vulnerable to the Holy Spirit first and to one another. When a lover in marriage is being vulnerable through prayer, emphasizing with your partner, validating their feelings, and giving them emotional support is a key part of some of the couple's prayers being answered.

Remember, praying for one another is giving and receiving at the same time. To receive support, one must be willing to give support also. Pray together as long as health allows you to. So that your intimacy resembles the intimacy of CHRIST and the church.

Chapter 23: Brag on Your Spouse and GOD to Edify and Not to Create Jealousy

During the spring and summer seasons during graduation and commencement ceremonies, we very well will commonly hear, "Said Person's name" followed by, "That's my baby or my son or daughter!" The same is to be said during a sporting event in which a parent's child is participating in. In both instances, the parents are celebrating what belongs to them.

If you were to visit any school ground or playground, any child would be glad to tell you about or introduce you to their parents. In their own way, it is a form of celebrating their parent(s).

Whatever the circumstances, parents and children feel special and celebrated when their people take the time out to brag on them. The celebrated one must maintain a level head in order to keep one ounce of pride from creeping in.

To speak proudly or happily about is the definition of brag. There are so many things that we can brag on. But whether we choose to or not, it may be of some significance to our marriages.

When men are together with other men and women are together with other women, both species talk about a wide range and variety of things. The talk can range from the positive and negative about the kids – the changes of life, and the challenges of life too.

In society, when the conversation begins about spouses, the negative outlook or negative energy seems to arise and pollute the environment. Let us take a look at some things and see how the negative energy can be reversed.

The scripture says, "Love is patient, love is kind. It does not envy, it does not boast". The outlook according to the scripture as well that we should articulate is by, "Giving honor to where and whom honor is due." If we are honoring, it doesn't feel like a brag.

We give honor to GOD for the blessings that are seen and unseen. Mahalal is a Hebrew word that means "Praise" and is sometimes translated as "Boast". Boasting in the Lord involves us giving glory, praise, and honor to GOD for who he is and the good things he has done. If efficiently approached, honoring and praising GOD for the attributes that he's blessed your spouse with to bless you and others with is in the Will of GOD! It's also edifying the work of GOD and the Kingdom.

We all at times desire to feel valued and be desired. Being that the enemy is a known influencer to inject the "What have you done for me lately?" spirit into marriages often, it should beseem us to radicate deeply in showcasing our valued spouse behind closed doors and openly as well.

In our proven nature, when we value something, we talk about it. We will value a restaurant that does not even belong to us, we talk about it. Value a store, we talk about it. Love how a car drives, we value and rave about it. Whether the restaurant, store, or car is around us or not, we talk about it.

If you are out and about and even if your spouse is or isn't in the group when you talk about him/her, it will make an enormous impact. It will impact the people and direct their focus toward the positive and it will (eventually) make your spouse feel valued and appreciated because that type of vibe is contagious and gets surfaced around.

Passing this contagious spirit around is part of your fruit which will multiply. Being fruitful and multiply can also have context as far as winning souls to Christ and not just for bearing earthly children. Did you know that how you edify GOD by edifying your spouse too, is an awesome way to let your light shine before couples so that they may see your good works and glorify the Father which is in Heaven"?

Fruit and fruit bearing produced in and through marriage are valued treasures. Those fruits can produce, create, multiply, and inject life into broken marriages, struggling marriages, or into the soon-to-be married couples.

These days, many people do not care to be examples. But just as bearing fruit in general or the lack thereof, bearing fruit can produce good fruit or bad fruit. As a people, whether we desire to be an example or not, our fruit or lack of fruit when it comes to marriage will determine or result if we're a good example or bad example as well.

We should never testi-lie, because only what's truthful and from the heart will eventually find a way around to reach the heart. Plus testi-lies have to be covered up and can be easily uncovered. Grow your fruit by speaking well of your spouse. But make sure it is in the way of thanking GOD for what you have in your spouse and valuing them as well. Not as in "Look what we got." There is no greater feeling after praising and pleasing GOD, than being responsible for being the one to edify your spouse's inner man or woman.

Chapter 24: Maintain What You Have and Don't Look Back

Earlier in Unit 2, we briefly discussed how we don't apply self-control when it comes to things in marriage, finances, and life. For a typical paradigm, notice how easy it can be to finance something or invest in something. After achieving it or obtaining it, one may discover that it is extremely more difficult or may feel that there is more pressure concerning maintaining it.

This saying comes up often and applies to this journey, "Each new higher level brings about new devils." Meaning that in this case, your marriage has now been established. But the persistent master of evildoers will still try to aggravate marriages and cause spouses to lose a little grip of the traction that has been built to this point.

Although not perfect, enough momentum should have been built by now. Momentum isn't classified, measured, or based on one occurrence, one juncture, one action, or one substance of significance. But relatively by continuous samples of correct behaviors and corrected wrong behaviors over a wide range of time.

By now, both spouses should know how to guard and protect each other. They should have developed a kind of back-to-back "us against the world" type of trust. Quite naturally if the biblical guidelines have been exercised effectively, these components should have also been fully matured at this time: Care, Commitment, Trust, Compassion, Communication, and Compromise. Although compromise can be good, marriages can not afford to compromise their traction, their momentum, their future, or unfortunately damage their good fruit.

This tedious road of poor execution of compromising traction will leave recently thriving marriages stuck on Salt Avenue if they are not careful. Woe unto that husband or wife that looks back or turns back to issues, behaviors, or things that GOD has freed and delivered them from that allowed the marriage to be able to flourish.

As the scripture told us in Luke 17:32, "Remember Lot's wife" in regard to the story of what happened to Lot's wife in Genesis Chapter 19. GOD's angel warned not to turn or look back, but Lot's wife looked back and was immediately turned into a pillar of salt. It stopped her progress, stopped her growth, turned her into stone, and stopped her being.

We can't move forward if we're constantly looking back or if we're considering looking back. When a train is moving forward full steam ahead, a train can accomplish and cover a great radius of distance as long as the tracks have been evaluated and aligned properly. Any obstacle or misaligned track can derail a train. The same is to be expected with your "Marriage Train". As long as the "Marriage Train" is moving full steam ahead, don't allow the enemy to derail your marriage especially at this point.

Maintain what GOD has built through the two of you and grow it further. If either one of you look back for any other reasons besides thanking GOD for where he has brought your marriage from, the marriage's growth can stunt and will in all likelihood cause a relapse in your marriage by causing a crack in the foundation and structure of your marriage. Regardless at whatever upper echelon stage that the marriage may be at, a crack is where it starts. Be watchful at all times, even holding fast to the fact that we are to prepare for war in the time of peace. Because our adversary will fight us until his time of torment has come.

Chapter 25: Handle All Necessary Business and Finish Strong

Whenever you see a thriving enterprise or business, someone once made a courageous commitment. Some conclude that the best time to plant a vision was in the past or probably years ago. But the second-best available time that we have is now. This inspiring quote by Walt Disney has been around for years. Disney said, "The way to get started is to quit talking and begin doing."

Planning is somewhat of an acquired skill. Often the skill set needed for planning can be grown or developed with a little practice and teaching. It is so easy to assume that life will venture or sort itself out and view planning as something that cripples the spontaneity of life. While there are places and a timeline for spontaneous action, there is also utility in prudency.

Being able to carefully control and cover your basic needs while painting a plan for the future often eliminates a variety of stress and tension in marriage. How can this be done? Sit down and have a very honest, open talk about what you both want, as far as you can imagine into the future. Have discussions frankly about finances, children, flexibility, future security, who will care and tend for the children, what you will be willing to sacrifice and compromise on, and everything else that is critical to you in building a happy life.

Understand that GOD may have something different in mind. GOD is the master planner, and he never makes mistakes. For the faithful, the future is one of grace, glory, hope, love, mercy, and much more. In the Bible, Paul's letter in Romans 8:24 depicts and is addressing primarily the believers, telling us to live in anticipation, hope, and excitement for our future in GOD's glory. Indeed, we are living in anticipation, but there are things and certain levels of business that GOD expects for us to have taken care of.

According to a U.S. Census Bureau report back in 2016, 24.4% of people 65 and older are widowed. Unfortunately, there are many cases where persons under the age of 65 that are also widowed. No one likes to think of the prospect of living life alone without their spouse, yet statistics tell us this is something we all should take the time to question and contemplate about valid answers.

Both spouses should be prepared in the event of the unexpected death of their spouse. Although we may not be prepared emotionally, we should have business setup and taken care of in all other areas to ensure that we have left our spouses in the best position to be successful if and when we are no longer around.

First Corinthians 14:40 instructs us to, "Let all things be done decently and in order." This same principle should be examined and established in our thought processes when it comes to putting our spouses and families in the best possible position for the future.

Here's a nugget. A Last Will and Testament is structured to protect you and your family when it comes to health and financial decisions in the event that you or your spouse are unable to make decisions. It also gives peace and legal structured details surrounding the events that are to take place in the event of sickness and death as far as medical decisions, funeral services, financial ramifications to assets and where they're to be distributed to and to whom, in addition to lowering the potential for family disputes. If no Will and Testament is in place, your family may be forced to spend excessive amounts of money to lawyers and the court system to settle these disputes in Probate Court for months on up to years in some cases. Know that if your spouse's name is not on a bank account, deed, title, or important paperwork in the event of death, with no Will and Testament in place, the living spouse will be forced to fight for it or lose it to the deceased spouse's estate.

If we by chance for any circumstance aren't able to accumulate the means of "Millionaire or Billionaire" status or what not as others, acquiring a Life Insurance policy will be able to give the surviving spouse and offsprings peace of mind in the inevitable event of enduring grief at the same time.

Some people say, "Well I'll be gone, so they'll figure everything out". But even in death, we have an obligation to uphold a part of our covenant with GOD. Even in preparing for death, CHRIST JESUS made the pathway straight for the disciples and others by directing, instructing, and by setting things in order for everyone to be able to flourish and carry-on once his time had come to an end. He also made it of importance of completing the necessary business of his father before his end time.

With the loss of the spouse, the household bills like rent, house notes, taxes, insurance, energy bills, etc., can become quite overwhelming. This is why it's imperative to prepare for and have our business straight, since we're unable to prevent the event of death.

This is where Life Insurance kicks in. There are plenty of benefits that can be received by having an insurance policy. Some prior to death and some after. Without life insurance, you may find yourself relying on the support of others after you've stopped earning an income while living. Help remove the burden from your family by making life insurance a priority when it comes to retirement.

It's your loved ones that are left to pick up the pieces surrounding the event. While you may not be able to comfort them emotionally, securing a life insurance policy will help your family be prepared for the financial situations that they encounter. Do not let pride and the unknown keep you from protecting the people you love.

Life insurance is not something to be indecisive about or undoubtedly take lightly, principally if you have young children or adult children. The first clause of Proverbs 13:22 says, "A good man leaveth an inheritance to his children's children:" After all, their financial future may depend on whether or not you have a secure plan for them. Without life insurance coverage, your children's basic needs, financial, and educational support may suffer. By chance if your children happen to be grown, leaving an inheritance to their children would be in order too.

Trusts are important as well. But pay very close attention! If a trust that has been put into action does not list the trust as the beneficiary of you or your spouse's life insurance policy, it will be considered as a piece of paper with no merit. Please know that the household that was running on two incomes has now been reduced to one after death. In the case of two Social Security checks, the survivor now gets to keep the bigger check, but the second goes away.

Not having things squared away is a simple but crucial wile of the devil. Life is not certain, but death is assured. Just as JESUS did, we are to give those loved ones around us dedicated effort and energy to supply them with comfort, direction, and the means to proceed efficiently emotionally, financially, and spiritually when we're no longer around. Supporting family and leaving an inheritance is not just financially speaking only. We have been endorsed and endowed with the power to leave an inheritance spiritually as well. We are to handle business in decency and orderly. Let us put our spouses and families ahead of death instead of putting them behind. Be a legacy and leave one too!

Chapter 26: Finish Strong and Be Happy

"This race is not given to the swift nor the strong, but to those who endure to the end"

People who are classified as impatient, are chiefly people who consistently stand firm on getting things taken care of or done now and at times become discouraged, disgruntled, and aggravated when time is stalled or wasted. However, there are some things that just can't be simply rushed. The development of a marriage is something that simply can not be rushed.

We were created perfectly in the image of GOD. Sin is what separated us from GOD, and we've been striving for perfection ever since. Because of this, there are not any perfect marriages. But if the wiles of the devil are avoided consistently, couples will discover that their marriage has been built to be perfect enough for them.

Almost anything exceptionally successful or good in life takes patience, time, dedication, and perseverance. If the lack of patience arises, a person is more likely to give up on marriage, dreams, goals, and other valuable things that at one point were important to them.

At one point or another in life, this phrase may have been heard; "Good things come to those that wait". But I've observed over time that most good things that do come, don't happen immediately or right away. Not desiring to zone in on what matters most importantly in this life often drives in impatience. Focusing on not-so-important things actually fuels impatience in abundance. In marriage, it fuels it so much that it interferes with focusing on the positive things, changing things, not leaving out how it confuses spouses into determining if they've been successful or have failed at any given point.

Success is not final; failure is not final or fatal: but the courage to continue and endure is theoretically what counts. When in any challenge, some say; "It always seems impossible when they're going through". But the key to the matter is action, "going through"! A mentor of mine, Pastor Leroy Hurst often instilled, "The only way we can lose on this journey is by giving up"!

Make it work. If both married participants have the desire to have a long lasting marriage that GOD intended for couples to benefit from, "make it work." Proverbs 18:21 tells us, ""Death and life are in the power of the tongue: and they that love it shall eat the fruit thereof." Romans 4:17 coincides with the power that the tongue has in which we are to, "calleth those things which be not as though they were."

Married Couples have the power to fight for their marriages. What GOD has ordained; he can surely maintain. But what are the two that are in the marriage willing to do.

With this chapter being the 26th way to fight against and escape the wiles of the enemy, understanding that we can not fight with physical weapons is part of the battle. "The highway of the upright is to depart from evil: he that keepeth his way preserveth his soul." (Proverbs 16:17) Meaning in marriage, spouses should not be fighting one another or the enemy with evil. By keeping, using, and by applying GOD's way, is what will at length preserve the couple's souls and marriage.

Although we've vaguely chatted about a few of these verses throughout the other chapters, let's focus on these 8 verses in Ephesians in their entirety to connect all of the dots. For it tells us and states,

"10 Finally, my brethren, be strong in the Lord, and in the power of his might.
11 Put on the whole armour of God, that ye may be able to stand against the wiles of the devil.
12 For we wrestle not against flesh and blood, but against principalities, against powers, against the rulers of the darkness of this world, against spiritual wickedness in high places.
13 Wherefore take unto you the whole armour of God, that ye may be able to withstand in the evil day, and having done all, to stand.
14 Stand therefore, having your loins girt about with truth, and having on the breastplate of righteousness;
15 And your feet shod with the preparation of the gospel of peace;

16 Above all, taking the shield of faith, wherewith ye shall be able to quench all the fiery darts of the wicked.
17 And take the helmet of salvation, and the sword of the Spirit, which is the word of God:

Through The Apostle Paul, GOD spoke plainly as to how we are to properly dress to protect ourselves against the devil and his tricks. The sword of the Spirit, which is the Word of GOD, is broken down further in Hebrews 4:12, "For the word of God is quick, and powerful, and sharper than any twoedged sword, piercing even to the dividing asunder of soul and spirit, and of the joints and marrow, and is a discerner of the thoughts and intents of the heart."

GOD's word according to Ephesians is a protector and gives an offensive edge according to Hebrews. Psalms 119 said, "Thy Word is a lamp unto thy feet and a light unto thy path", to show us which paths to avoid. But how do we defend ourselves? Through the Word of GOD. In Solomon's Letter in Ecclesiastes 7:12, it rightfully says, "For wisdom is a defence, and money is a defence: but the excellency of knowledge is, that wisdom giveth life to them that have it."

GOD has given us everything to walk through this journey of life with, especially in marriage. He's left no stone unturned or untouched and has eliminated every excuse for marriages to be dying off these days at such a rapid pace. Wisdom giveth life and it ties in with happiness. "He sent his word, and healed them, and delivered them from their destructions". Psalms 107:20

If you're already headed for destruction, the enemy doesn't have much to do. But if there's a calling on your marriage, he sees what GOD has in store for you two. There are blessings that he has for us individually and there are blessings that he has for couples. The devil can not curse what GOD has blessed, but the scheduled to be blessed couple can forfeit blessings before GOD releases them by being a willing participant outside of the "Will of GOD".

Hockey great Wayne Gretzky once concurred, "You miss 100% of the shots you don't take."

Take the shot at finishing strong and at being happy. You'll never reach it if you never try or take the shot.

Don't worry about what you've been through. Just focus on happiness and focus on finishing strong. This is a marathon, and GOD has given spouses everything that is needed to fulfill his natural purpose-filled agenda for marriages and for the Kingdom. If couples properly understand, support, and be obedient to his agenda, married couples will reap all of the benefits and enjoy a healthy and vibrant long-lasting marriage.

When the enemy comes to steal, kill, and destroy the marriage; do what JESUS did and speak what is written. Speak life that, "The devil can not...... The devil will not....... Have your marriage.

In the words of another one of my mentors, "Pastor Duke Chance", "The second half of your life is about to be the best half of your life" If the words are slightly switched up, "The second half of your marriage will be the best half of your marriage."

Read the WORD...... Believe the WORD......Obey the WORD......Speak the WORD...... Spread the WORD...... Apply the WORD to life and marriage and we'll see you and your spouse happily still together at the finish line; as you two have Escaped Twenty -Six of the wiles of the devil by finishing strong!

"The grace of our Lord Jesus Christ be with you all. Amen."
Revelations 22:21

Quotes/ References/ Recognition

Quote: Benjamin Franklin
Quote: Rev. Jermaine Young Sr.
   (Uncredited) Don't Crack Under Pressure
   (Uncredited) Shortcuts That Lead to Dead Ends
Quote: Walt Disney
Quote: Pastor Leroy Hurst Jr.
Quote: Wayne Gretzky
Quote: Pastor Duke Chance

Reference: Holy Bible (KJV)
   (NLT)
   (AMP)

Recognition/ Support: April Young

Made in the USA
Columbia, SC
29 October 2024